D0575670

MADE IN GREAT BRITAIN

Aiden**Byrne**

NEW HOLLAND

CONTENTS

FOREWORD BY TOM AIKENS

Where do I start? Aiden and I have known each other for well over ten years now, working together for about four of those. We've been through a lot together and have had some great times – Aiden is one of the closest friends I have as a chef. We have shared and talked about everything to do with food and it is this understanding of and passion for food that has brought us together. It has shaped his life and made him the great chef that he is today.

It all started when Aiden came to work with me at Pied à Terre back in 1996. I will admit that at that time I was a very, very demanding chef that worked all my staff extremely hard. I would stop at nothing to get the best from them and worked them harder than I really should have. But Aiden just kept on going and never stopped or wilted under the extreme pressure of working beside me. He was my number two and he just would not stop till the job was done the exact way that I had asked and wanted from him – with never a word of complaint. He would come with me to Covent Garden vegetable market at 3.30am, then we would go straight into work for 6am, pack everything away and then do a full day's work till 1am. We were working six days a week then – myself, Aiden and three other chefs in the kitchen for almost nine months. It was unbelievable that we ran that kitchen with just four or five chefs. This is where he helped me keep the two stars at Pied à Terre and without him there I realise that this could and would have been an impossibility. I am truly indebted to Aiden and what he did with me back then.

He came to work with me again as my head chef at Tom Aikens for a further two years and here I really pushed him to his limits. He knew what I wanted and what we had to do; I could not have asked any more from a person. When I think back I was the luckiest man alive to have Aiden with me, and I don't think he has realised – even today – how much I value all that he did. The pressure I put him under and the stress of the work never fazed him, tough scouser that he is. The man would never buckle, but just get stuck in and push on. He understood the reasons why we did these crazy hours and why we worked so hard. We both share an old-fashioned belief that with hard work and determination anything is possible. To have someone like him as your right-hand man is priceless. He worked without question and with total dedication.

Running a kitchen is about forming relationships with your team and fellow workers, but especially with your number two. It can be very difficult trying to combine a working relationship with a friendship as you have to keep the balance between serious work and light-hearted kitchen banter. I know that there were times when I demanded too much from Aiden but he never complained. He was always the first one in and the last one out.

You may all wonder what drives us crazy chefs to work the hours we do but with Aiden it genuinely is a passion for excellence. I believe this makes him stand out from a lot of other chefs. Working under huge amounts of pressure gives you standards, procedures, schooling, dedication and understanding. I relied on Aiden more than anyone else. Every place you go to work you take something with you, be it the way the chef works, the style of food or the way the kitchen is run. Eventually you find your way, your style and your food. With the understanding of all this you will make your mark and Aiden has certainly done this. It makes me very proud to see how far he has come and to see him challenging himself and his team in such a positive way. We can all take the easy routes in life and we can all follow other people but to be a leader and to stand on your own two feet takes a huge amount of effort and hard work.

Aiden has come full circle in his career and he now has chefs looking up to him and coming to work in his kitchen because of him, his food, his style, his personality and his own drive and dedication. I will never forget the times we have had and shared together. There were great times and hard times but it was the way we worked together, the way he made it all worthwhile and how he motivated my staff that I thank him for. I have a lot of great memories and sometimes I do get nostalgic for the old days when we did service together and could practically read each others minds. I miss that and if ever the opportunity came along again for us to work together then I would jump at the chance. There has never been anyone else like him, but I will always have his friendship and that's invaluable.

Introduction

INTRODUCTION

British food has for a long time had a pretty bad press, unfairly, in my opinion. But it does, in fact, have an extremely rich and varied history that stretches right back to Roman times. And there is so much fantastic produce that is available to us in Britain. True, British food and cooking has had its low points but many people today are beginning to rediscover good food and recognise that it is at its most tasty and healthy when fresh and in season. In towns and cities across Britain, farmers' markets, selling produce grown or made locally, have become increasingly popular. What's great about these markets is that you can talk to the producer while he or she wraps up your purchases. All this has been accompanied by a rekindled interest in cooking and a backward glance at old family favourites.

In this book I have attempted to show you how the best British ingredients can still be combined to create an outstanding British cuisine that rivals the best in the world. British cuisine has really come a long way in the last few years but in London the change has been remarkable. London has long been a dynamic centre of food fashion and there are now hundreds of fantastic restaurants – many of them serving world-class food.

Today, there is no reason why good British cooking can't be the rule, rather than the exception – and not just in London's fashionable restaurants. I'd like to see great British food in restaurants right across the country – and more importantly, in people's homes and kitchens.

Today's British food scene

When I was a young chef, things were very different as far as produce was concerned. It arrived at the door, we opened the packaging and did what we needed to do to it: seasoned, marinated, cooked it and made it look pretty on the plate – at least that was my understanding. The main priority was to make the customers smile, leave happy and tell their friends. Then the restaurant would stay busy and I'd keep my job.

Now, almost 15 years on, things have changed dramatically. I have, I hope, a little more knowledge and a lot more respect; respect for the clientele, respect for my staff and most importantly respect for the produce.

If I were to have written this book ten years ago, it would have been destined for the professional chef, but now, that is not the case. Times have changed. Cookery books like this have replaced designer magazines and autobiographies as a coffee table staple. As a chef that is an amazing change to witness and be a part of.

Actually, ten years ago I would not be able to write this book unless I had three Michelin stars and a chain of restaurants to my name. People are now looking for more variety, are keen to try new ideas. They want to push their culinary boundaries – not just by what they eat in restaurants but in their homes. Knowledge and information are key and that information is in demand more and more.

The work that has taken place to change the stigma of British food is slowly paying off. We are well on our way to being respected around the world. Back when I started out, top restaurants were the only ones championing traceability of produce, and as time has gone on this approach has filtered down to gastro pubs, farmers' markets and even the big supermarkets.

Fantastic produce is now available to everyone. You just need to invest time in shopping around. We can all be a little lazy and just accept what is placed on the supermarket shelf irrespective of what is in season, what is local, what is British. Perhaps our supermarkets don't want their customers to think seasonally, because they believe seasonality is not profitable?

Luckily for chefs – and those of you who cook for pleasure at home – we have farmers' markets, family-run butchers, fishmongers, cheese shops and an endless list of specialist suppliers to choose from.

There are still plenty of small producers in this country dedicated to the art of cultivating the very best varieties of seasonal, British produce. These fruits, cheeses, meats, and vegetables have not been genetically improved for the sake of shelf life, nor inoculated for long-distance travel. Food bought in this way represents only a small handful of all that we buy. We must all continue to make an effort to change and as long as we keep chipping away there is still hope. Perhaps one day one supermarket will dare to be different and find a way to sell seasonal British produce and still make the huge profit their share-holders demand. Let's hope so.

The making of a chef

I always knew that cooking at this level was going to be hard, but never this hard. Once I started cooking everybody told me I was mad. Why do you work so many hours for such little money? Why do you put up with all the abuse? I didn't have the answers because I didn't understand it myself. Still to this date I don't recall the day when it went from obsession and adrenalin to actually being my career, something that was going to provide for my family and make me feel important and worthy of something.

I feel extremely lucky that when I was just 14 years old I found my vocation, my passion, my life. I owe a lot of my determination to my dear cousin and friend Alan Feeney. I suppose he was like my big brother, he chose catering in school and I copied him and that was it, there was no turning back.

At catering school, I got a real taste of what was going on in the outside world. At weekends and public holidays I used to travel to Wilmslow in Cheshire and work for free in a hotel called Stanneylands. Iain Donald was the executive chef. He both frightened and excited me. He was mad. He spoke fluent French in a very strong Scottish accent and grown men were obeying every order that he shouted. The service ran like clockwork. It was here that I thought, 'This is where I want be'. Fifteen years on and my brother Louis, who is also a chef, now works for Iain Donald.

So college finished and off I went to the big smoke. I hated every minute of my first short visit and vowed never to go back. I didn't learn a thing; it took the wind out of my sails. I hated my job and my world was shattered.

I came home and headed to the Chester Grosvenor hotel. I heard it had a Michelin star; the Arkle restaurant was impossible to get into, so I worked for free until a position became available. Here I started to learn how to respect ingredients, how to cook vegetables properly, how to be organised and efficient.

I stayed here for 18 months and learned as much as I could until I heard of another Michelin starred restaurant not too far away, called Pool Court Restaurant in Otley (West Yorkshire). Here I learned how to taste; the senior chefs would ask me to taste their food to see if it was seasoned properly – I now insist all my chefs continuously taste what they are cooking. It was here that I met my best friend Roger Hickman. We went through everything together: the head chef used to make us cry on a daily basis. I guess that was his way of getting the best out of people, by filling them with fear, but it's a tactic I disagreed with then and one I disagree with now. A pat on the back or a 'well done lad' will stay with someone that young and naive for a very long time. I remember him whispering in my ear 'I was better than you when I was 20', but I was to have the last laugh.

The way I treat my staff now is very important to me, mainly because of the way I was treated for all those years. My chefs work four days on and three days off. Of course they put in a full week's work for the four days but at least they can

experience a life outside the kitchen. They receive credit where credit is due and a detailed explanation when they have made a mistake.

After Pool Court I packed my bags and off I went again on my travels, avoiding London like the plague. I ended up in Norwich, in a small family restaurant called Adlard's. To say I was wet behind the ears is an understatement. I didn't understand why mousses were splitting, why my anglaise was lumpy. I had never cooked a piece of meat before. With what little money I had, I bought cookery books by Harold McGee, Raymond Blanc and Marco Pierre White. These are what spurred me on and I loved it. I had my own little domain.

I think other than David, the chef/proprietor, I was the only one who had worked in a Michelin starred restaurant. David was trying to bring up two very young children at the time, and when he was not in the kitchen the standards plummeted. One day I told him he needed to employ a sous chef; he gave me the responsibility and I ran with it. I went into work on Monday mornings and came out on Sunday mornings. I had no life, no friends, and no money. I put into practice what I had learnt from previous Michelin starred restaurants and studied my cookery books.

After about nine months, David received a phone call from a journalist friend to say congratulations, 'for what?' said David. 'For getting your lost Michelin star back'. Ours was the first restaurant in the country to have done this at the time. And I was the head chef! I didn't really understand the importance of this until I went to the Michelin dinner at the Savoy hotel.

I had to wear a dinner suit; I had never even worn a suit before let alone a dinner suit. It got even more bizarre for me when I arrived for dinner. Standing in front of me were John Burton Race, Raymond Blanc and Brian Turner to name but a few. My chin was on the floor. I kept pinching myself, 'can this be true?' All my idols, the authors of all these books, all in one room and I'm here receiving a Michelin star for Adlard's.

I stayed with David Adlard for 5 years, but I needed to learn more, so I bit the bullet and went back to London. But I am eternally grateful to David for giving me that first opportunity.

I set up camp next with Richard Neat who was the head chef of Pied à Terre in London, which had two Michelin stars. The kitchen was a dungeon, literally. It was a million miles away from my safe little domain in Norwich, everyone wanted to be the best, no matter what it took. I lasted six months and committed the ultimate cardinal sin. I bolted.

Then Tom Aikens took over as head chef and I was encouraged to come back. Never have I met one person who has so much drive and ambition. Tom, without a shadow of doubt, has been the biggest influence on my career. We have stayed strong friends through thick and thin. It is difficult to say how I feel about Tom; he still makes me nervous but at the same time I couldn't imagine my life if Tom hadn't come into it.

Soon it was time to move on again, and after five years in Dublin at The Commons restaurant (where I picked up another Michelin star), I was called by Tom Aikens to return to his eponymous restaurant as his head chef. Even though I was now 30 years old, with a wealth of experience behind me and two separate Michelin star awards, I can honestly say that this was the hardest period of my career. Tom pushed me to the limits but I always saw the value in what he was doing. I knew that by going back I was taking one step back to jump two steps forward.

My arrival at The Dorchester in Park Lane, London, as head chef was an enormous privilege and since 2006 I have achieved so much with the help and support of an immensely talented and dedicated team of chefs. The facilities are incredible and have enabled me to grow, distil and concentrate my ideas further as a chef.

Cooking at home

I consider myself extremely lucky because not only is cooking my passion but it is also my job – it's what I get to do every day. Working in a professional kitchen means that I have access to some of the best ingredients this country has to offer. It's a privilege to work with some of my regular suppliers (see the features in individual chapters) and I know that it is easy for me to source the best seasonal produce around. I also have a team of willing chefs on hand, as well as all the equipment a professional kitchen has to offer.

I do realise that you won't have all this at your fingertips but this doesn't mean that these recipes can't be attempted by any domestic cook with a love of good food and a willingness to experiment. The recipes in this book are by no means set in stone and although I have included them in all their glory, as I would serve them in the restaurant, there is no reason why you shouldn't adapt, add or remove elements as you wish. The recipes should be used as a guideline and it is down to the individual to use their own taste buds and initiative when making a dish. When seasoning dishes the aim is to let the main ingredient shine through, with other flavours coming through and complementing it. Seasonings such as salt, pepper, sugar and lemon juice are as useful and necessary as a good set of knives and a good cook will learn how to use them to best effect.

Vegetables

This dish is a great summer starter. A gazpacho is meant to have some acidity, but you also need to taste the earthiness of the beetroot, which is why the recipe includes some raw beetroot. However, you also want to taste the natural sweetness of the beetroot, which is why some of the beetroot is baked. The idea is to have the perfect balance of acidity with sweetness and saltiness coming through.

Chilled Beetroot Gazpacho with Vodka Jelly and Avocado Sorbet

SERVES 4
2 kg fresh beetroot
2 large golden beetroot
1 vanilla pod
50 ml olive oil
300 ml fresh apple juice
500 ml beetroot juice
125 ml sherry vinegar
juice of 2 lemons
2 whole avocados
100 g caster sugar, plus extra
    for seasoning
juice and rind of 2 limes
juice of 1 lemon
2 leaves gelatine, softened
200 ml Belvedere vodka
salt
fresh coriander, to garnish

WRAP HALF THE BEETROOT and the golden beetroot in foil, place on a tray lined with rock salt and cooked in a preheated oven at 160°C/310°F/gas 2½ for 1–1½ hours. Leave them to sweat in the foil for 10 minutes – this will make them easier to peel. Peel the golden beetroot and use a small cutter (1.5 cm in diameter) to cut four pieces of beetroot. Peel the other cooked beetroot, cut four more pieces and chop the rest up into small pieces. Scrape the seeds from the vanilla pod and mix with the olive oil. Store the beetroot fondants in this oil.

PEEL THE REMAINING raw beetroot, chop the flesh into small pieces and place them in a blender with the cooked beetroot, the apple juice and the beetroot juice. Blend until smooth, then pass the liquid through a fine sieve by tapping the sieve; don't try to push the pulp through the sieve, because you only want the juice. Put the liquid in a bowl over a bowl of iced water.

SEASON THE SOUP WITH SALT, gradually adding more and more until it tastes right. Then add the sherry vinegar, which will almost accentuate the salt. Then add some sugar, which should balance both the flavours. Pass again through a fine sieve and refrigerate. You will probably need to test the seasoning again once the gazpacho is fully chilled.

PEEL THE AVOCADOS and use the same cutter to cut four shapes out. Coat in lemon juice and set aside. Add the sugar to 100 ml water and bring to a boil. Blend the rest of the avocado in the blender and add the syrup. Pass through a fine sieve and add the lime juice and rind and the lemon juice. Transfer to an ice cream machine and churn until frozen.

HEAT A COUPLE of tablespoons of water in a small saucepan, add the gelatine and a small amount of the vodka and leave the gelatine to dissolve slowly. Remove the pan from the heat and add the remaining vodka. Pass the jelly through a fine sieve into a small container and set in the refrigerator for a couple of hours. It will go cloudy; do not worry.

TO SERVE, recheck the seasoning of the soup and pour it into four chilled bowls. Add the fondants, spoon in some vodka jelly and avocado sorbet and garnish with a few coriander leaves.

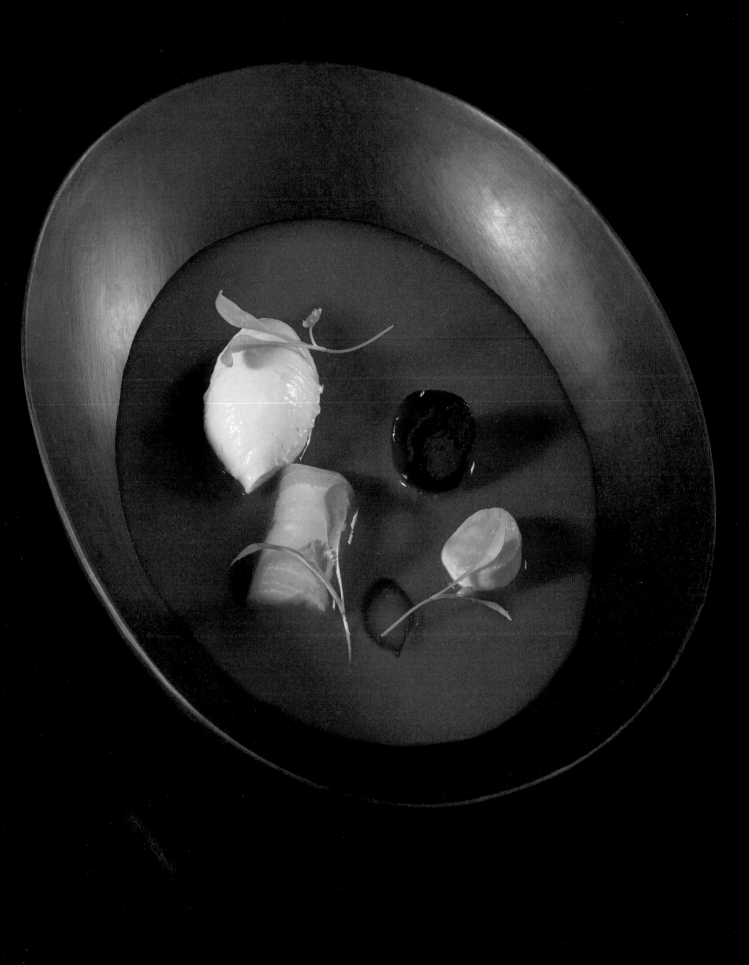

This is a perfect winter soup that I think is a lot easier to make than the classic French onion soup. I like to serve it with veal shin ravioli or a crisp crouton spread with some chicken liver and foie gras parfait. Remember: the younger the onions, the sweeter the soup.

White Onion and Parmesan Soup

SERVES 4
3 kg new season white onions
3 large sprigs of thyme
25 g butter
2 litres boiling white chicken stock
  (see page 199)
200 ml double cream
50 g very finely grated Parmesan
juice of 1 lemon

PEEL AND SLICE the onions as finely as possible, ideally using a mandolin. (The thinner you slice the onions, the quicker they will cook and the fresher the soup will taste.)

IN A WARM, covered pan slowly sweat the onions and thyme in the butter for 20–30 minutes until the onions are transparent and very soft. If you cook them too quickly they will not taste as sweet as they could, and if you cook them too slowly they will taste stewed. The idea of sweating is to cook them as quickly as possible to retain the freshness. So keep tasting every 5 minutes or so. Add the boiling chicken stock, bring back to the boil and add the cream. Return to the boil again and then blend in a blender.

WHILE THE SOUP is in the blender add the Parmesan. Be careful when you reheat the soup because the cheese tends to catch on the bottom of the pan. I add the Parmesan as if I'm adding salt, literally using it as a seasoning. Also be careful about adding salt to the soup because Parmesan is often very salty.

PASS THE SOUP through a fine sieve, then chill immediately to retain the freshness. If like, add a dash of lemon juice to finish the soup. Reheat gently to serve.

This is a perfect recipe for Christmas, which also works as a sauce for pheasant, turkey or even a firm piece of fish, such as turbot or Dover sole. The foie gras ravioli are simply for garnish – pan-fried ceps also work well. I like the soup as it is because it's so moreish. Fresh chestnuts are definitely best. You can use precooked vacuum-packed ones, but they tend to be a bit sweet, so reduce the amount of Madeira to counterbalance the sweetness.

Chestnut Soup with Foie Gras Ravioli

SERVES 4

RAVIOLI
120 g raw foie gras, diced
10 ml sherry vinegar
2 tablespoons shallot confit
  (see page 210)
2 tablespoons finely shredded
  flat leaf parsley
75 g chicken mousse (see page 214)
100 g fresh pasta (see page 208)

SOUP
150 g fresh or vacuum-packed
  chestnuts
75 g shallots (peeled and sliced)
3 sprigs of thyme
25 g unsalted butter
75 ml white wine vinegar
100 ml Madeira
600 ml hot white chicken stock
  (see page 199)
200 ml double cream
salt

FIRST MAKE THE RAVIOLI. Season the diced foie gras with salt and fry in a hot pan until golden brown. Transfer to a plate, drizzle over the sherry vinegar over and put in the refrigerator until chilled. Mix together the diced foie gras, the shallot confit, the parsley and the chicken mousse and leave in the refrigerator for a couple of hours until it is firm. Put a large pan of boiling water with a dash of olive oil on the stove and have a bowl of iced water ready and a slotted spoon.

FEED THE FRESH PASTA through a pasta machine a couple of times on each setting, gently pulling the pasta as it goes through the machine. Take the machine down to the very finest setting and feed the pasta through at least three more times. Dust your work surface with flour, cut the sheet in half and brush half with some water. Spoon the mixture onto the wet sheet and then lay the dry sheet on top. Use a pastry cutter to cut out 4 ravioli and seal with your fingertips, making sure that all the air is forced out. Cook the ravioli for just a couple of minutes. Remove from the pan with a slotted spoon and plunge into the bowl of iced water. Drain, then drizzle with a little olive oil and refrigerate.

MAKE THE SOUP. Peel the chestnuts by piercing the dark husk. Run the point of a small knife along one side, then simply peel back the husk. An easy way to remove this is to dip the chestnuts, one at a time, into boiling water and then scrape it off while the chestnut is still warm. Slice the chestnuts as finely as possible.

IN A WARM COVERED pan sweat the shallots and thyme in the butter until the shallots are soft and transparent; do not let them colour. Season with salt, add the sliced chestnuts and cook, covered, for a further 5 minutes over a low heat; again, do not let them colour. Add the white wine vinegar, increase the heat and reduce until almost dry. Add the Madeira, reduce until dry then add the boiling stock. Bring the mixture back to the boil, then add the cream. Return the mixture to the boil, remove the thyme and then blend in a blender. Pass through a fine sieve and into a bowl over iced water to chill. Check the seasoning.

REHEAT THE SOUP and pour it into four soup bowls. Reheat the ravioli in a pan of boiling water and drop them into the soup.

The two main ingredients in this soup are in season at exactly the same time. It is an old Spanish classic, Ajo Blanco, which can be served hot or cold. Fresh almonds can be difficult to source, even when they are in season during the summer months (July to October). When they are available I like to make the most of them. The apple jelly gives a good acidic undertone, but you could, if you like, garnish the soup with white grapes.

Chilled New Season Garlic and Almond Soup with Granny Smith Jelly

SERVES 4
2 kg new-season green almonds
2 kg new-season wet garlic
1 litre full-fat milk
100 ml single cream
50 ml sherry vinegar
100 ml dry sherry
150 ml Greek yogurt (optional)
sorrel or oxalis leaves, to garnish
salt

APPLE JELLY
7 granny smith apples
juice of 1 lemon
2 gelatine leaves, softened
100 g caster sugar

TO SHELL THE ALMONDS you will need a small tack hammer, a wooden chopping board and a steady hand. It's best to use a tack hammer because you don't want to crush the almonds, just crack the shell. This may take a bit of getting used to, but it's worth being patient. As soon as you have shelled the almonds, blanch them in boiling salted water for about 10 seconds and plunge them immediately into iced water. This makes it easier to peel away the brown skin, leaving you with a bright white almond. If you can't find fresh almonds toast 150 g flaked almonds just long enough to release the oils and flavour. Drop them into the cream to infuse with a drop or two of almond extract or oil.

PEEL THE GARLIC. This will be easier than peeling normal, aged garlic because the skin will almost fall away. Put the garlic in a saucepan and cover with one-quarter of the milk. Bring to the boil, simmer for 5 minutes and then drain the milk away. Cover with another quarter of the milk and repeat the process until all the milk has gone. Once cooked, the garlic should be so soft that you can almost squash the cloves between your fingertips.

PUT THE GARLIC, almonds and cream in a saucepan. (If you are using almond-flavoured cream drain away the almonds and cover the garlic with the cream.) Heat and simmer for 5 minutes, stirring until smooth.

PASS THE MIXTURE through your finest sieve and chill immediately over a bowl of iced water. If you are going to serve the soup cold, wait until it's chilled before you season. If you are going too serve it hot, season it before chilling. Season with salt, sherry vinegar and dry sherry. The sherry vinegar and the dry sherry will cut through the richness and give the soup a really fresh taste. If you are serving it cold it will benefit from a little Greek yogurt being mixed in just before you serve.

MAKE THE APPLE JELLY. Peel six of the apples and keep the skins separate. Juice the apples in a vegetable juicer and transfer the liquid to a saucepan. Bring the juice to the boil, remove from the heat immediately and pass through a muslin cloth or very fine sieve. You will have a clear apple juice. While the juice is still hot put it

in a blender with the reserved apple peel and blend until the juice is bright green. Add a squeeze of lemon juice, the gelatine and the sugar. Strain again into a bowl set above iced water. When the jelly begins to set slightly transfer it to the refrigerator for at least 2 hours. Finely shred the remaining apple.

TO SERVE, pour the soup into bowls (chilled if the soup is cold) and spoon some jelly in the centre. Garnish with shredded apple, sorrel leaves or, as here, oxalis leaves, which have a similar flavour to Granny Smith apples.

GROWING BABY SALADS IN WILTSHIRE

I firmly believe that vegetables, herbs and fruits are a cook's greatest asset. Any cook who thinks vegetables are the least interesting part of a meal, a bore to prepare, and a mere garnish to meat or fish, is totally missing the point. As far as I'm concerned, vegetables are a staple, central to a dish, the real deal. A lot of my dishes are based around fruits or vegetables – meat, fish or dairy is quite often an afterthought, something to fill the dish out.

Today there really are no excuses for not using organically grown fruit and vegetables. I could almost guarantee that if you were to have your vegetables delivered each week by one of the many box schemes working hard to change the way we think about organic produce, you would spend the same amount of money as you would do filling your stainless steel trolley on a Saturday afternoon. Plus, it would make you think a little more about what you cook, and you would discover new flavours and combinations.

Food miles (how far your carrot, potato or apple flew, aided by fossil fuel, in order to sit on your plate) is a big issue for enviromentalists. I try to buy British produce when it's in season but when I have to I choose imported produce from a source I know is benefiting the people growing it. Britain could be much more self-sufficient and not import out-of-season produce from far flung places – but only if the supermarkets were prepared to pay a fair price for them. Also, if Britain's farmers grew a greater variety of crops, they would live less under the threat of abandonment by supermarket buyers.

Greengrocers are fast disappearing from the British high street. They find it too much of a struggle to compete on price with the supermarkets. If you have a greengrocer near you – support it! They buy their produce straight from the traditional wholesale market, who buy straight from the grower. This simple supply chain means you can buy vegetables that were picked the previous afternoon, and you will taste the freshness. Again it's a question of pester power; ask your greengrocer to sell the vegetables and fruit at the time of year you want them and when they are at their best.

However, it is not all doom and gloom as smaller chains of supermarkets build long-term relationships with farmers. Some support watercress growers in the South, and rhubarb growers in Yorkshire. Others encourage farmers to grow specialist vegetables such as wild mushrooms, violet pearl aubergines and spiny artichokes. I would love to see fields of artichokes growing in Yorkshire and sweet peppers in Devon's greenhouses.

A true ambassador to the cause is someone who has been a great friend of mine for almost ten years, Richard Vine from R.V. Salads based in Wiltshire. He is the maestro of all things very small. Richard's passion is now centred fully on growing micro salads after a career as a livestock producer and organic vegetable producer. He now runs a highly successful operation supplying England's best restaurants with ingredients that simply were not available seven or eight years ago.

Born and raised on his family farm in Berkshire, in a world where everyone foraged for nature's seasonal harvests and grew a large proportion of their own food, he experienced massive changes in food production, and consumer expectations of it. In a world where nothing was wasted, food was both British and seasonal, with national pride in his produce being taken by producers and consumers alike.

Richard says, 'the myriad of convenience and fast foods, with a whole fusion of taste experiences from around the world meant that we as a nation came very close to loosing both our national and regional food heritage'.

Richard's business needed to diversify to meet the demands from a new breed of chef whose passion and desire to source and use every available British product was unbounded. He operates in both a greenhouse and an outdoor environment where the skills and dedication of his small team of passionate and committed gardeners and pickers reign supreme. Everything from ground preparation to seed sowing and produce picking is all done by hand.

The philosophy is to work in partnership with nature and so his crops are subject to fluctuations in temperature, humidity and daylight. There is also the inevitable problem of pests. They try very hard not to use any form of pest control, preferring to dispose of crops (composting what they can) and starting again. If absolutely necessary he uses an organic control method.

Greenhouse heaters are set on frost control only (this is his small attempt at conserving fossil fuels and reducing his carbon footprint). Each tiny plant and leaf is packed with phenomenal flavour as well as being aesthetically beautiful. Visual appearance and taste are of equal importance and it is exciting to see how these qualities marry with and enhance any dish. It usually takes him eighteen months to find out if a new plant or leaf is viable.

Some of Richards's favourite micro salads that I include on my menu are:

Nasturtium: hot and peppery
Watercress: peppery
Buckler sorrel: sharp/citrus/apple
Red chard: sweet/mild beetroot
Yellow chard: strong/earthy beetroot
Chicory italica rosso: bitter/dandelion
Mizuna: delicate mild/cabbage/hint of mustard
Russian kale: sweet/cabbage/earthy
Red mustard: mild cabbage/then increasing mustard flavour/heat
Bronze fennel: sweet/increasing/intense aniseed
Green fennel: sweet/mild delicate aniseed
Broad bean and runner bean flowers: delicate/tastes exactly like the baby pods/tiny hint of sweet pollen

If you have the inclination, time and space there is also another way you can get closer to the joys of eating fresh vegetables all through the year and that is by growing it yourself. For the truly committed there are allotments but you can produce quite a lot in a small garden or even on a balcony using growbags and containers. As a busy chef I am not the one to tell you how to do it. But I know that it's a worthwhile exercise and worth exploring if you can. To witness the changes in the garden throughout the year must make you think about food in a different way. If you have nurtured something from seedling to maturity you will really appreciate its value.

You can really do anything with vegetables, but remember the biggest sin of all is overcooking. Vegetables picked young and fresh from the garden need barely any cooking or no cooking at all. Old stale vegetables, or those that are cooked too long, not only loose the high proportion of vitamins and minerals that are in vegetables, but become dull and tasteless as well.

Every month of the year there is something new arriving at my kitchen door to get me motivated and excited. The dishes that go on the menu in the restaurant are constantly changing as we celebrate the seasons and incorporate vegetables that are at their most tender and flavoursome. Britain is capable of providing outstanding vegetables and if you keep your ear close to the ground and badger your suppliers for seasonal produce you will reap the rewards.

Richard Vine is the master of micro salads in England. I've been fortunate enough to have known him for almost ten years. I've wanted to pay homage to Richard for a long time by creating a dish based around his gorgeous nasturtiums. The watercress-like pepperiness of the nasturtium leaves is an excellent counterpoint to the pickled cockles and capers. The pickled cockles are best prepared at least a day in advance.

Richard Vine's Nasturtium Salad with Pickled Cockles, Red Mullet and Capers

SERVES 4
75 ml white wine vinegar
10 white peppercorns
100 ml white wine
3 large sprigs of thyme
6 bay leaves
1 onion, roughly chopped
4 garlic cloves, sliced
1 kg fresh cockles, rinsed in cold water for 2–3 hours to remove any sand
150 g potato, peeled and finely sliced
pinch saffron strands
2 egg yolks
200 ml vegetable oil, plus extra for frying
juice of 1 lemon
30 medium-sized nasturtium leaves
24 multicoloured nasturtium flowers
75 g ready-made tempura batter mix (available from Asian food stores)
4 small red mullet fillets, scaled and pin-boned
olive oil, for tossing
1 large banana shallot, sliced into rings
2 teaspoons superfine capers
salt and pepper

MAKE THE PICKLING liquor. Put the white wine vinegar and white peppercorns in a saucepan with half the white wine, half the thyme sprigs and half the bay leaves in a saucepan and simmer for 5 minutes. Leave to cool and season with a little salt.

MIX THE ONION with the remaining wine, thyme and bay leaves and half the garlic. Heat your largest casserole-style pan for 5–6 minutes and add the drained cockles and the onion and wine mixture. Cover and cook for 3–4 minutes.

POUR THE COCKLES onto a tray and allow them to cool slightly (reserving the cooking liquor). Pick the cockles out of their shell and put them straight into the pickling liquor. Leave them in the liquor for as long as possible, up to 24 hours.

MAKE THE SAFFRON cream. Strain the liquid in which cockles were cooked through muslin or a very fine sieve place into a saucepan with the remaining garlic and the sliced potato and the saffron. Cook until the liquid is almost gone. While it still warm add the egg yolks and, using a whisk attachment on a hand blender gradually add the oil, as if you were making mayonnaise. Season with salt and lemon juice and set aside.

MAKE UP THE BATTER according to the directions on the packet. Coat a quarter of the nasturtium flowers, leaves and cockles in the batter and fry in hot oil until crisp. Season with salt and lemon juice as soon as they come out of the fryer.

SEASON THE FISH fillets and cook in a nonstick frying pan, skin side down, for about 1½ minutes until the skin is crisp. Turn the fish over and cook for a further 30 seconds. Season with lemon juice and cut each fillet into 3 pieces.

TO SERVE, put some saffron cream on each plate. Toss the remaining cockles in a little olive oil and scatter them over each plate. Add the deep-fried cockles, flowers and leaves, and then sprinkle over the remaining leaves and flowers. Add the capers and shallot rings and finally scatter over the fish fillets.

The trick with this recipe is to make the watercress stay as green as possible. Watercress is at its best in the summer months, and the English season runs from March to September. Like rocket, goats' cheese and sun-dried tomatoes, watercress has suffered lately from having become rather trendy, but I still think it's one of the most satisfying and vibrant leaves there is.

Watercress Soup with Poached Cod and Hen's Egg

SERVES 4
1 litre whole milk
1 garlic clove, halved
4 large sprigs of thyme
1 kg cod fillet
75 ml fish stock (see page 200)
100 ml double cream
2 kg watercress
1 large potato, peeled and finely sliced
1 large onion, peeled and finely sliced
25 g butter
1.5 litres boiling vegetable stock (see page 198)
4 large organic hens' eggs
75 ml white wine vinegar
2 tablespoons chopped chives
salt
cracked pepper

BEFORE YOU START have a large bowl of iced water ready with another large bowl (preferably stainless steel) sitting on top of it so that you can chill the sieved soup immediately and keep its freshness and colour. Fill your deepest saucepan with water and bring to a high boil.

HEAT THE MILK with the garlic and thyme sprigs, remove from the heat and leave to infuse. Meanwhile, season the cod with salt and cracked pepper. After 15 minutes return the milk to the heat, put the cod in the milk and allow it to cook slowly for 2 minutes. Remove from the heat and leave the cod until the milk cools. Remove the fish from the milk and flake it onto a plate. Set aside.

PUT THE FISH stock in a saucepan and heat to reduce by half. Add half the double cream, reduce the liquid again by half and keep warm.

PICK THE LEAVES from the watercress stalks. Sweat the onion and potato together in the butter in a covered, heavy-bottomed pan, making sure that they do not colour. If the potato sticks add a little vegetable stock and remove the stuck potato with a wooden spoon. Cook until the potato is soft. Add two-thirds of the watercress leaves and cook for a further 2 minutes. Add the hot vegetable stock and return to the boil. Add the rest of the cream and reboil. Transfer the mixture to a blender and blend in batches until smooth. Add the remaining watercress as you blend; this will give a fresher soup, in both flavour and colour. Pass the soup through your finest sieve into the bowl set on iced water then immediately transfer to the refrigerator.

CRACK THE EGGS into four separate cups and turn down the boiling water to a low simmer. Add the vinegar and drop the eggs in one by one. (I don't whisk the water, because if you have enough water the eggs should form teardrop shapes on their own.) Cook the eggs for 1½ minutes and plunge them into iced water to stop cooking.

TO SERVE, gently reheat the soup. Reheat the cod flakes in the fish cream and add the chopped chives. Reheat the poached egg in hot water. Put the soup in four bowls, spoon in the creamed cod and top with a poached egg.

This is a perfect vegetarian starter that would also serve two as a light lunch. It's quite a substantial dish and has a very strong flavour.

Tomato Confit and Braised Lettuce Tart with Braised Lettuce and Courgette Purée

SERVES 4

1 carrot
1 shallot
1 garlic clove
4 sprigs of thyme
4 baby gem lettuces, cut in to quarters lengthways
300 ml vegetable stock (see page 198)
1 packet ready-made puff pastry
2 quantities tomato confit (see page 210)
10 large torn basil leaves
1 kg courgettes
10 g butter
20 g grated Parmesan cheese
baby basil cress, to garnish
salt and pepper

PEEL AND ROUGHLY CHOP the carrot, shallot and garlic, put them in an ovenproof pan and cook to slightly caramelize. Add the thyme sprigs and place the lettuce on top. Cover with the vegetable stock, bring to the boil, season with salt and pepper and cover. Braise in a preheated oven at 140°C/275°F/gas 1 for about 1 hour or until the lettuce is soft.

MEANWHILE, roll out the pastry and cut 4 circles 4 cm across. Any unused pastry can be frozen for use later. Place the circles between two baking trays (see page 46) and cook in a preheated oven at 180°C/350°F/gas 4 for 20–25 minutes. Remove the top baking tray and cook for a further 5 minutes. Allow to cool on a wire rack.

LINE FOUR SMALL blini pans with clingfilm and layer the tomato confit 'petals' in the bottom, leaving an overhang of tomato pieces to fold over later.

WHEN THE LETTUCE is cool chop it fairly coarsely, mix in the torn basil leaves and pack into the blini pans on top of the tomatoes. Once the tart is full, fold the petals back over to seal in the lettuce. Allow to sit for a couple of hours.

USE A SMALL knife to peel away the skins from the courgettes. Discard the flesh and finely chop the skins. Cook the skins in a warm, covered pan with the butter until they are soft. Season and transfer to a blender. Blend until smooth, pass through your finest sieve and chill immediately over a bowl of iced water.

TO SERVE, reheat the tomato and lettuce in a steamer. Turn it out on the tart bases, sprinkle Parmesan over the tomato and put in a preheated oven at 180°C/350°F/gas 4 for 10 minutes. The cheese will melt, the base will stay crisp and the tart should be piping hot. Warm the courgette purée through and spoon a little onto each plate and garnish with the baby basil cress.

The main ingredients in this recipe are at their best at roughly the same time of year. The creamy pine nuts, the sweetness from the ripe peaches, the pungent flavour from the basil and the acidity from the tomatoes make this a well-balanced summer starter. Look for peaches that have a yellow or creamy colour (these will be the sweetest) and avoid any that are too soft because they will spoil very quickly.

Tomato and Peach Salad
with Pine Nut Vinaigrette

SERVES 4
2 large Heritage tomatoes
  (any colour)
4 ripe peaches
25 g caster sugar
3 leaves gelatine, softened
4 cherry tomatoes
50 g pine nuts
25 ml sherry vinegar
100 ml olive oil
50 ml double cream, semi-whipped
1 handful of baby basil
salt and pepper

USE A 2 CM diameter pastry cutter to cut out four fondant shapes from one of the tomatoes and from one of the peaches. Put these in the refrigerator.

CHOP THE REMAINING peach and put the flesh in a saucepan with 50 ml water and the sugar. Cover and cook for about 5 minutes or until the peach is soft. Add the gelatine and stir to dissolve. Transfer the mixture to a blender and blend until smooth. Pass the liquid through a fine sieve and allow to set in a bowl in the refrigerator.

MEANWHILE, plunge the cherry tomatoes in boiling water for no more than 10 seconds, remove and plunge immediately into iced water. The skins will peel away easily.

SLIGHTLY TOAST the pine nuts, chop them and mix them with the sherry vinegar and the oil. Season with salt and pepper and set aside.

WHEN THE PEACH jelly is set fold in the whipped cream until it is fully incorporated and return to the refrigerator.

CUT THE REMAINING tomato into four slices and arrange them on four small salad plates. Dress the cherry tomatoes and the peach and tomato fondants in the pine nut vinaigrette and arrange them next to the tomato slices. Spoon some peach mousse onto each plate, sprinkle over the basil and dress with a little more pine nut vinaigrette.

If you've already made a batch of beetroot purée for a recipe this is another great way to use it. This can be served with a main course, such as roasted venison, or simply as a starter on its own. Alternatively make the risotto in advance, let it go cold, roll into small balls and coat with a tempura batter and deep-fry – perfect as canapés.

Beetroot and Vodka Risotto

SERVES 4
100 g Parmesan cheese
50 ml white chicken stock
   (see page 199)
1 quantity risotto base
   (see page 209)
½ quantity beetroot purée
   (see page 204)
vodka, to taste
lemon juice (optional)
salt (optional)

GRATE 75 G of the cheese and shave the remaining 25 g with a vegetable peeler.

IN A LARGE, flat-bottomed pan heat the chicken stock and reheat the risotto in the hot stock. Fold in the beetroot purée and grated Parmesan and add the vodka to taste. If liked, adjust the seasoning with a touch of salt and a dash of lemon juice.

SERVE IN four bowls scattered with the shaved Parmesan.

This basic, rather rustic dish can be served in the finest of restaurants and will be appreciated by the most discerning of diners. I use De Cecco macaroni tubes (Zita .18) which you will find in good Italian delicatessens. I also use frozen peas for the purée – they give a fresher, sweeter taste than fresh ones because you don't have to cook them for so long. It's also worth spending a few extra pence on good-quality frozen peas.

Parmesan Macaroni with Peas and Ricotta Gnocchi

SERVES 4
100 g frozen peas
300 ml vegetable stock
  (see page 198)
60 g butter
1 quantity ricotta gnocchi
  (see page 208)
100 g Zita .18 macaroni tubes
1 quantity of béchamel sauce
  (see page 205)
50 g Parmesan cheese, grated
2 egg yolks
300 g fresh peas
4 asparagus spears
2 tablespoons chopped chervil
1 tablespoon of chopped dill
pea shoots or chervil, to garnish
salt and pepper

MAKE THE PEA PURÉE. Put the peas, 100 ml of the vegetable stock, the butter and some seasoning into a pan and bring to the boil. Transfer immediately to a blender and blend until smooth. Pass through your finest sieve into a bowl over iced water to keep the colour.

PREPARE THE RICOTTA gnocchi as on page 208, adding 50 g pea purée to the mixture. Cook and set aside.

FILL YOUR LARGEST, deepest saucepan with water, add a dash of olive oil and plenty of salt and bring to boil. Cook the macaroni for 11–12 minutes, then plunge immediately into iced water to chill. Drain and dry on a clean tea towel. Chop the macaroni into 2 cm dice, and fold the pieces into the béchamel sauce, three-quarters of the Parmesan and the egg yolks. Season with ground pepper and salt. Transfer to four small buttered earthenware pots and cook in a preheated oven at 180°C/350°F/gas 4 for 15 minutes.

POD AND BLANCH the fresh peas in plenty of boiling salted water for 4 minutes. Plunge the cooked peas into iced water to stop the cooking. Trim the asparagus (see Asparagus Mayonnaise, page 49) and slice the spears on a mandolin. Blanch them in the same water as the peas for a seconds then plunge them iced water.

REHEAT THE REMAINING vegetable stock in a pan and mix in the remaining pea purée. Add the ricotta gnocchi, the fresh peas, the asparagus and chopped herbs and reheat until warm. Serve on a separate plate next to the macaroni and garnish with pea shoots or chervil.

I sometimes serve this dish with some soused mackerel or pan-fried red mullet. Both the mousses can be used as different garnishes, and the yogurt sorbet is also used as a dessert accompaniment. It is definitely best to make these mousses and sorbet first thing in the morning and allow them to set during the day. The tuilles need to be made the day before.

Beetroot and Avocado Mousse with Yogurt Sorbet

SERVES 4
400 g beetroot purée
  (see page 204)
50 g caster sugar, plus
  1 tablespoon for the mousse
juice of 2 lemons
4 gelatine leaves, softened
200 g crème fraîche
3 ripe avocados
1 teaspoon vitamin C powder
1 quantity yogurt sorbet
  (see page 219)
salt and pepper

MAKE THE BEETROOT TUILLES. Heat 200 g beetroot purée with the sugar until the sugar has dissolved. Leave to cool slightly and check the seasoning. You are looking for the sweetness from the sugar but also for a hint of acidity. Add a little lemon juice until you can just taste it.

PUT AN OVENPROOF rubber mat on a baking tray and spread the beetroot mixture over the mat with a palette knife as evenly and thinly as you can. Place in an oven as low as you can possibly have it to dry the tuille out overnight. (If you have a gas oven with a pilot light hold the door slightly ajar with, say, a wooden spoon.) When the purée is dry enough you should be able to peel it away from the mat as a whole sheet. If you cannot, you will need to dry it for longer.

WHEN IT IS READY use scissors to cut it to your desired shape. The tuille needs to be soft, pliable and slightly warm for you to do this. As soon as it cools it will become crisp. You can warm it again slightly to soften it. Keep the tuilles in a cool, dark place.

MAKE THE BEETROOT MOUSSE. Warm the remaining beetroot purée in a saucepan. Transfer 2 tablespoons of the warm purée to a smaller pan, add half the gelatine and stir to dissolve. Add this mixture to the larger amount of warm purée (this will make sure that the gelatine is evenly incorporated).

TRANSFER THE PURÉE to a stainless steel or glass bowl set over a bowl of iced water. Adjust the seasoning, bearing in mind that you want the natural sweetness of the beetroot to come out. Add a touch of acidity with some lemon juice and even a little salt. When the purée has set fold in half the crème fraîche.

CHECK THE SEASONING again and adjust if necessary. Cover the bowl with clingfilm and place in the refrigerator to set. (It will keep for two or three days.)

MAKE THE AVOCADO mousse. Peel, stone and chop the avocado and put the flesh in a blender. Dissolve the vitamin C powder in 120 ml cold water, add to the avocado and blend until smooth. Pass the mixture through your finest sieve. Reserve 4 tablespoons for serving.

WARM 2 TABLESPOONS of the purée, add the remaining gelatine and heat gently until the gelatine has dissolved. Add this mixture to the remaining purée and season with salt and a tablespoon of sugar. Transfer to a bowl set over iced water and fold in the remaining crème fraîche. Put a piece of clingfilm directly on top of the mousse and transfer to the refrigerator to set.

TO SERVE, spoon the reserved avocado purée on to four cold plates. With a spoon warmed in hot water, scoop a quenelle of each mousse onto each plate, then add spoonful of yogurt sorbet and place a tuille between two of the mousses.

David Adlard was one of my first true mentors, and I am eternally grateful to him for giving me my first opportunity as a head chef. Some of the dishes I learned as a young chef have stayed with me throughout my career and David's version of this classic potato dish is one of them. You can't prepare this in advance and it does monopolise your oven but it's well worth it. Perfect with sirloin steak, béarnaise sauce and some fresh green beans.

David Adlard's
Potato Dauphinoise

SERVES 4
400 ml full-fat milk
300 ml double cream
2 garlic cloves
3 large sprigs of thyme
2 large waxy potato, such as
  Desiree or Cara
150 g Cheddar cheese, grated
salt and pepper

PUT A SHALLOW baking tray with some water in it in the oven. Preheat the oven to 80°C/180°F/gas ¼.

PUT THE MILK and cream in a saucepan with the garlic and thyme and heat. Leave for 20 minutes to infuse, stirring occasionally to stop it from catching on the bottom of the pan.

PEEL THE POTATOES and slice them on a mandolin as thinly as possible. Put them in the warm cream mixture and cook until the potatoes are just tender. Take care that they do not catch and burn.

POUR THE CREAM and the potatoes into large colander resting over another saucepan. Continue to cook the cream gently until it coats the back of a wooden spoon. Season with salt and pepper.

LAYER THE POTATO slices in an ovenproof earthenware dish, sprinkling the grated cheese between each layer. Season with salt and pepper every other layer and add a small ladleful of the cream every third layer. When you have layered all the potatoes, cover with the remaining cream, sprinkle a final layer of cheese on top and wipe the sides of the dish. Put the potatoes into the tray that is in the oven, standing it in the water, which should come to the top of the dish. (The water will stop the cream from boiling; if it boils with the cheese in it will separate.) Cook for at least 3 hours. The potatoes will colour gradually. Serve when they are golden brown.

Ceps and aubergines are a marriage made in heaven. I use this combination in lots of different ways – with monkfish, lamb or just as a wonderful vegetarian starter like this one. If you like, you could put some pickled anchovies on this tart.

Tarte Fine of Aubergines and Ceps

SERVES 4
4 sheets of filo pastry
100 ml olive oil
4 thyme sprigs
3 onions, peeled and finely sliced
4 large sprigs of thyme
50 g butter
250 g cep mushrooms
6 baby aubergines
2 garlic cloves, sliced
50 g Parmesan cheese shaving
buckler sorrel leaves, to garnish
salt

MAKE SURE THAT YOU always keep filo pastry covered with a slightly damp tea towel so that it doesn't dry out. You will need two heavy, cast-iron baking trays, preferably the same size. Put a sheet of greaseproof paper on one of the trays, and place the first piece of filo on this. Brush it with a little olive oil, sprinkle with a small amount of salt and then scatter over one-third of the thyme leaves. Put a second sheet of filo on top and repeat the process, then add the third and fourth sheets in the same way. Brush the top with olive oil and cover with another piece of greaseproof paper. Put the second baking tray on top of the filo 'sandwich', making sure that the pastry is fully covered, and put a weight on top. Bake in a preheated oven at 140°C/275°F/gas 1 for 20–25 minutes. Remove from the oven. When the pastry is crisp, transfer to a wire rack and allow to cool.

IN A WARM covered pan sweat the onions, thyme sprigs and a sprinkle of salt with the butter until the onions are very soft. Remove the lid and continue to cook for a further 30–40 minutes until the onions begin to caramelize. When the onions are golden brown, check the seasoning: you should be able to taste the salt but the natural sweetness of the onions should also be evident. Transfer the onions to a tray to cool down then set aside. (I keep a jar of onions at this stage in the refrigerator to use in other recipes. You will find that if you don't drain away the butter it will act as a preservative.)

SLICE THE MUSHROOMS and the aubergines evenly lengthways so that you can see their natural shape and then pan-fry them both in olive oil with a few garlic slices and a sprinkle of salt until golden brown. Drain onto a wire rack and leave to cool.

SPREAD THE ONION lyonaisse over the tart and layer the aubergines and ceps on top, piling them up as much as you like. Top with the shaved Parmesan and bake for a couple more minutes in a preheated oven at 180°C/350°F/gas 4. Serve the tart with a crisp sorrel salad and some more Parmesan shavings.

This is a dish we came up with a couple of years ago, and it appears on the menu only in the asparagus season, when it sells like hot cakes. It's a play on the classic recipe, and at the restaurant we pair it with smoked bacon and with morel mushrooms, which are in season at almost the same time as English asparagus. If you wish, you can simply serve the poached asparagus and the mayonnaise foam.

Asparagus Mayonnaise

SERVES 4
4 large duck eggs (or hens' eggs if you prefer)
12 spears of English jumbo asparagus
4 very thin slices of strong smoked pancetta
50 g unsalted butter
1/2 bunch of chervil, chopped
4 tablespoons Hellman's mayonnaise
4 slices of smoked bacon
olive oil
lemon juice
salt
toasted bread, to serve

In the restaurant we use a gas canister to create an asparagus foam – simply put the mayonnaise mixture into a gas canister and charge with two cartridges. Shake well and leave in the refrigerator for about 2 hours. When ready to serve, pipe some mayonnaise from the canister into each bowl.

STEAM THE DUCK EGGS for 7 minutes (hens' eggs for 6 minutes) in a steamer that is set as high as possible to give evenly cooked yolks. Plunge the cooked eggs into iced water and leave them to chill. Peel away the shell and keep in the refrigerator.

DIVIDE UP THE ASPARAGUS: you will need four tips for pan-frying, four for slicing and four for the purée for the mayonnaise. Trim the leaves away from the asparagus that will be pan-fried, starting from the bottom. The base of the spear is too tough to eat, so hold the very base and the centre in both hands and bend it until it snaps. Discard the lower section. Plunge the four spears into a large pan of boiling salted water for 1–2 minutes or until the asparagus is slightly undercooked. Transfer to iced water and allow to cool, them dry on kitchen paper and wrap each spear in a slice of smoked bacon. Set to one side.

TRIM A FURTHER FOUR SPEARS. Slice the asparagus lengthways on a mandolin, starting from the base. Use only perfect slices. You will need four slices per portion. Blanch in boiling salted water for a couple of seconds, then plunge into iced water and dry on kitchen paper.

CHOP THE REMAINING asparagus and any discarded slices. In a warm covered pan sweat the asparagus in 25 g butter until soft (this should take 3–4 minutes). Add a pinch of salt and the chopped chervil and cook for a further minute. Blend until smooth then pass through a fine sieve. Cool immediately in a bowl over iced water, then leave in the refrigerator for a couple of hours until the mixture stiffens. Fold in the mayonnaise, then leave to sit in the refrigerator for 2 hours.

COOK THE BACON-WRAPPED asparagus in a frying pan with the remaining butter until golden brown. Keep warm.

TO SERVE, warm the eggs in a steamer for a couple of minutes. Dress the asparagus slices with a dash of olive oil, some lemon juice and salt and arrange them in four bowls. Place a spoon of mayonnaise into each bowl, cut the top of the eggs and place an egg in the centre of the mayonnaise. Arrange the pan-fried asparagus on the side with a small piece of toast to dip into your egg.

Fish

What I love about this dish are the small bursts of sea saltiness provided by the caviar. If you can, shop around for live prawns; frozen ones are definitely a second-grade choice for this dish. Also look for the largest prawns you can find. You can prepare the individual components of this dish in advance to make serving easier. Use the heads and the claws of the prawns to make langoustine stock.

Roasted Dublin Bay Prawns with Broccoli Purée and Ricotta Gnocchi

SERVES 4
12 large live Dublin Bay prawns
  (langoustines)
2 kg broccoli
olive oil
250 g ricotta
70 g 'oo' pasta flour
2 egg yolks
150 ml crayfish stock (see page 200)
75 ml double cream
juice of 1 lemon
2 teaspoons of beluga or oscietra
  caviar
1 punnet of baby basil cress,
  to garnish
salt and cracked black pepper

FIRST PREPARE THE PRAWNS. Do wear rubber gloves because live prawns have a tendency to nip your skin. Pull off the tail and then extract the intestine by holding the middle fin on the tail, twisting slightly and pulling gently. The intestine should come out as you pull.

BRING A LARGE PAN of water to a boil and have a bowl of iced water ready. Dip the prawn tails into the boiling water and quickly plunge them into the iced water. This is so you can remove the shell without damaging the flesh. Hold the prawn in the palm of your hand and squeeze slightly or until you hear the crack of the shell. Peel away the shell. Place the tails on kitchen paper in the refrigerator until needed.

MAKE THE BROCCOLI PURÉE. Shave the very green tips from the head of the broccoli with a small, sharp knife. Bring a large pan of salted water to the boil. Have a blender set up and have a bowl of iced water with another bowl inside. You also need a fine sieve. Put the broccoli shavings into the sieve and lower into the boiling water. Boil rapidly for 2 minutes, then carefully transfer the broccoli shavings to the blender, reserving a few small florets. Blend until smooth; if necessary add a little of the blanching water. Spoon the purée into the sieve and push through into the chilled bowl. Check the seasoning, then keep in the refrigerator until needed.

BRING A PAN of salted water to the boil and add dash of olive oil. Have a large bowl of iced water and a slotted spoon ready. In a bowl mix together the ricotta, flour and egg yolks. Season with salt and pepper. Use a teaspoon to form small dumplings and drop into the boiling water for about 2 minutes or until the gnocchi are firm. Transfer them to the iced water, drain and keep refrigerated, coated in olive oil.

MIX TOGETHER THE STOCK with 25 ml cream and heat to reduce by half. Add the gnocchi and broccoli florets to reheat. Add a dash of lemon juice and the caviar, stir gently and keep warm. Heat up the broccoli purée over a low heat. Fry the prawns in very hot olive oil until golden on all sides.

PUT SOME BROCCOLI purée on each plate, add prawns and gnocchi and pour the sauce over them both. Garnish with the baby basil cress.

This is a good, simple starter: make the purée, make the sauce and cook the scallops. It really is that easy. Ask your fishmonger to prepare your scallops for you. You only need the actual scallop meat for this recipe, so remember to keep and freeze the skirts.

Roasted Scallops with Apple and Ginger Purée with Fennel Sauce

SERVES 4
4 Granny Smith apples
200 g peeled fresh ginger,
  finely chopped
100 ml of double cream
2 fennel bulbs
300 ml vegetable stock
  (see page 198)
2 star anise
3 large sprigs of tarragon
10 medium sized scallops
25 g butter
juice of 1 lemon

QUARTER THE APPLES and discard the cores. Chop the flesh fairly roughly, put the pieces in a large saucepan with 300 ml cold water and add the ginger. Bring to the boil and simmer gently until the water has evaporated. Add the cream, then transfer to a blender and blend until smooth. Pass through a fine sieve and keep warm.

COARSELY CHOP the fennel and put the pieces in a saucepan. Add the vegetable stock, the star anise and the tarragon, bring to the boil and simmer for 10 minutes. Allow to cool and remove the star anise. Blend in a blender until smooth.

CUT THE SCALLOPS in half widthways and fry in olive oil in a large, hot, nonstick frying pan. They will take about 1 minute to caramelize on one side. Then turn them over and cook for a further 30 seconds, add the butter and cook for a further 30 seconds. Season with a few drops of lemon juice and transfer to a warm plate.

SPOON THE PURÉE into the centre of the plates. Place the scallops around the outside of the purée, five on each plate, then spoon the fennel sauce around the outside.

This dish is about as simple as I get, but the key is to make sure that you have the freshest possible scallops. It can be served as a starter or an appetizer, and the ingredients listed here are enough to serve four people as an appetizer. If you would like to serve it as a starter, increase the quantities in proportion to the increase in the number of scallops.

Scallops with Garlic and Lime Purée

SERVES 4
4 large hand-dived scallops
4 large heads of garlic, peeled
50 ml double cream
juice of 3 limes
1 Granny Smith apple (optional)
2 tablespoons olive oil
25 g butter
lemon juice
1 tablespoon lemon purée
  (see page 203) (optional)
wood sorrel or buckler sorrel,
  to garnish
salt

IF YOUR FISHMONGER has not done so, remove the skirts, roes, muscles and stomachs from the scallops. Keep the skirts, rinse them under cold water for a couple of hours and store in the freezer for use in another recipe.

PUT THE GARLIC in a small saucepan and cover with cold water. Bring to the boil, drain away the water and cover again with cold water. Reboil and again drain the water away. Repeat this process until the garlic is soft enough to squash in your fingertips. (Boiling the garlic like this will extract any bitterness.)

COVER THE GARLIC with the cream, simmer for 5 minutes and blend in a blender until smooth. Press it through your finest sieve, then whisk in the lime juice and season with a little salt.

LEAVING THE SKIN on, slice the apple on a mandolin and shred the flesh finely into matchstick strips.

CUT THE SCALLOPS in half widthways. Heat a large, nonstick frying pan and fry the scallops in the olive oil. They will take about 1 minute to caramelize on one side. Turn them over and cook for a further 30 seconds. Add the butter and cook for a further 30 seconds. Season with a few drops of lemon juice and transfer to a warm plate.

SPOON THE GARLIC AND LIME PURÉE into the centre of four plates. Brush the top of each scallop with lemon purée, if using, and place them on top of the garlic purée. Garnish with the sorrel and apple strips, if using.

I love this combination of ingredients, which ooze richness, sumptuousness and class. You have a choice here: cook your own lobster, which will ensure you have the freshest one there is (see note), or buy a ready-cooked one.

Lobster with Morels and Tarragon Gnocchi

SERVES 4
4 English lobsters, 500 g each
2 kg fresh broad beans
1 quantity potato gnocchi
   (see page 205)
leaves of 2 large sprigs of tarragon,
   chopped
2 large shallots, thinly sliced
50 g butter
1 bay leaf
2 sprigs of thyme
300 g fresh morels, cleaned
150 ml white wine
150 ml Madeira
300 ml white chicken stock
   (see page 199)
150 ml double cream
100 g tempura batter mix
   (available from Asian food stores)
juice of 1 lemon
salt

To prepare a live lobster you will need a large knife and a heavy chopping board. Put the lobster in the freezer for 15 minutes while you bring a large pan of water to the boil. Cooling the lobster prevents it from moving around while you're working, which is a lot safer. Place the lobster on the board with its back facing up. In the middle of its head are a line running up the middle and a line running across, forming a cross. Place the point of the knife in the centre of the cross. Thrust the knife straight down into the body. Slice down through the head.

BRING TWO LARGE PANS of salted water to the boil and have two large bowls of iced water ready. Put the lobster in one of the pans and cook for 6–7 minutes. Transfer immediately to a bowl of iced water. You may need to cook the lobsters one at a time.

WHEN THE LOBSTERS are chilled, remove them from the water and separate the tail from the body. Use a pair of large, heavy-duty scissors to remove the flesh from the shell. The underside of the lobster is the weakest point, so run the scissors under the shell. Prise the shell open and remove the flesh in one piece. To remove the meat from the claws gently prise the moveable pincer away from the main part of the claw; the inner cartilage will come out with it as well. Then tap the shell with the back of a knife until it cracks slightly and prise it apart. Keep the shell to make stock later.

SHELL THE BEANS and blanch them in the saucepan of boiling water for no more than 2 minutes and plunge into iced water. Set aside.

PREPARE THE GNOCCHI as on page 205, adding 1 teaspoon of diced tarragon leaves before rolling out and cooking.

IN A WARM PAN sweat the sliced shallots in the butter with the bay leaf and thyme sprigs until soft. Add the morels and cook for a further 2 minutes. Add 100 ml white wine and reduce until almost dry. Add the Madeira and reduce until the mixture is almost sticky, then add the stock and reduce by half. Now add the cream and reduce by 100 ml. Discard the thyme stalks and remove half the morels – set these aside. Blend the remaining liquid in a blender until smooth. Pass through a fine sieve and season with half the lemon juice and some salt.

HEAT A SMALL AMOUNT of the morel sauce separately and add the gnocchi, the reserved morels, the remaining diced tarragon and the broad beans. Warm the lobster tail and claw in some of the morel sauce. Put the lobster on four plates and simply spoon the gnocchi mixture around them. Warm the remaining morel sauce and spoon over the lobster. Make up the tempura batter and dip the claws in. Fry at 180°C/350°F until golden brown. Remove from the fryer, season with salt and lemon juice and serve with the lobster, morels and gnocchi.

This is a simple recipe with complex flavours. It's a good, basic winter soup or an appetizer for a gourmet meal. You could add poached quails' eggs and some apple dice as garnish. Do try to find a good source of smoked eel. Be careful with the amount of salt you use in this recipe because smoked eel can be salty.

Smoked Eel and Apple Soup

SERVES 4
3 Granny Smith apples, peeled and chopped
50 g shallot, coarsely chopped
25 g unsalted butter
4 large sprigs of fresh thyme
1/2 smoked eel (skin and bones), about 1 kg
500 ml boiling white chicken stock (see page 199)
100 ml double cream
juice of 1/2 lemon

PUT THE APPLES in a bowl of acidulated cold water to prevent them from discolouring.

IN A LARGE, warm, covered pan sweat the shallots with the butter and thyme for 2–3 minutes without letting them colour. Drain the apples and add to the shallots, stir and re-cover and cook for a further 5 minutes.

MEANWHILE, peel the skin from the smoked eel and remove the flesh from the bone simply by running your knife down both sides of the backbone. Leave the bone and the skin whole and add them to the apple. Re-cover the pan and cook for a further 2 minutes. Chop half the eel flesh and add this to the cooking apple.

ADD THE BOILING chicken stock and the cream, reboil and allow to simmer over a low heat for a further 3–4 minutes. Season with a little salt if necessary. Remove the skin, bones and thyme sprigs from the soup, and place the mixture in a large blender. Blend for 1–1½ minutes until it is smooth, then pass through your finest sieve and chill over iced water as quickly as possible to retain the freshness.

TO SERVE, reheat the soup. Dice the remaining eel and put it in the bottom of the bowls as garnish, adding add a dash of lemon juice to freshen the taste.

This is a refreshing dish, and it's also one that can be prepared well in advance. You'll get the best results when the mackerel is at its freshest, so befriend your fishmonger and ask him to let you know as soon as the mackerel arrives.

Carpaccio of Mackerel with Pickled Vegetables and Fines Herbes

SERVES 4
100 ml white wine
75 ml white wine vinegar
10 white peppercorns
20 coriander seeds
6 bay leaves
4 large sprigs of thyme
1 garlic clove, halved
2 shallots, peeled and halved
125 g carrots
3 celery sticks
100 g white button mushrooms
1 teaspoon of lemon thyme leaves
1 tablespoon chopped chives
4 large fresh mackerel
12 sprigs of chervil
salt

PUT THE WINE, vinegar, peppercorns, coriander seeds, bay leaves, thyme sprigs, garlic and shallots into a large pan and bring to the boil.

CHOP THE CARROT and celery into small dice the same size. Put them into the pickling liquor and bring back to the boil. Finely dice the button mushrooms (using only the white parts) so they are the same size as the carrot and celery, and add them to the saucepan. Then add the lemon thyme leaves and leave to cool.

FILLET THE MACKEREL by removing the head, slicing the stomach open and removing the guts. Wash under cold running water to rinse all the blood away. Run a sharp filleting knife down each backbone to remove the first fillet, turn the fish over and remove the second fillet. Run under cold water. Remove the pin bones with a pair of tweezers. Slice the fish as finely as possible and lay the slices on four cold plates.

ONCE THE VEGETABLES are cool, drain and mix in the chopped chives. Season with a little salt.

ARRANGE THE DICED vegetables around the sliced fish. Garnish with sprigs of chervil sprigs and a sprinkling of sea salt and spoon a couple of tablespoons of the pickling liquor over the sliced mackerel.

DIVING FOR SCALLOPS IN SCOTLAND

Britain has a lot of coastline and a lot of fish. Or rather, we had a lot of fish. Over the last 30 years the demand for fish and shellfish has doubled. While there is no doubt that some species in our coastal waters are in danger, there are still a number of stocks that remain healthy – the ones that come from well-managed and sustainable sources.

Unfortunately, there are too many fishing vessels chasing too few fish. Nearly all the fishing areas are open all the time and the effectiveness of the regulations that have been put in place, to govern the stocks, relies on the truthful reporting of catches and landings by all fishermen, and yet the temptation to misreport must be irresistible. The majority of fish stocks are either fished to full sustainable capacity or are overfished.

If I can avoid fish that is caught deep at sea in factory ships I will always endeavour to. Technology has played a major part in the problem of overfishing. The nets can be up to a mile wide and thanks to global positioning systems and sensors these ships can identify whole shoals and scoop them up into their hold, along with rare and endangered species. Their fish aggregating devices actually attract the fish into their nets.

So, just as we have made the conscious effort to increase the quality of the way our livestock are handled, and the way our fruits and vegetables are grown, the same efforts must be made to ensure our fishing is kept at a level where we are not running out. In fifty years' time we still want to be able to say, 'shall I have fish or meat this evening?'

You should be able to ask your fishmonger for the lesser-known types of fish, many of which are normally shipped abroad due to lack of interest here. These are the alternative species, the ones that have not been overfished and are just waiting to be discovered. There are plenty of fish species that are at safe biological limits, including John Dory, langoustines, mackerel, Dover sole and turbot. Just ask your fishmonger for advice.

However, there are certain species of fish and shellfish which, at the moment, are dangerously close to collapse. These include the popular haddock and cod to skate and fish from further afield, such as Chilean sea bass. Consult the Marine Conservation Society, who publish regular updates about edible species on their website www.fishonline.org.

I try to buy seasonal, inshore fish, line-caught by day boats. The fishermen who man single trip boats go out to sea for short periods of around 12 hours and as a result come back to port with the freshest fish. Besides the freshness of their catch and the fact they don't literally hoover up the seabeds, they also support local communities, employing local deckhands, boat builders and mechanics. A good fishmonger will enthusiastically articulate all there is to know about everything they sell, so do engage and make friends with him or her – you will reap the rewards.

We are still lucky enough to have a few fishmongers left on the high street along with fish stalls in markets. But they are fast disappearing as the supermarkets become more dominant. When I'm cooking for my family I always choose a trusted fishmonger over the supermarket fish counter. They have a larger variety of fish on offer and they also give you an opportunity to have a good look and chat to the fishmonger.

Another good solution is to buy direct from small-scale fisheries via the internet. Most of them sell direct from coastal towns and send their fish overnight, packaged in polystyrene boxes, guaranteeing the freshness a supermarket can't.

Of all the regions in the British Isles, Scotland must boast some of the finest produce and the fish on the west coast of Scotland is outstanding. Recently I was lucky enough to take a trip to visit a supplier and friend of mine, Kenny McNabb, who runs a company called Flying Fish. We travelled along the banks of the glorious Loch Lomond, the largest expanse of fresh water in Great Britain and the romantic centrepiece of the National Park, past the world-famous Loch Fyne and on to Tarbert in Argyll.

Kenny runs his fishing business employing freelance divers to hand pick the crustaceans from the seabed. Kenny's divers commit an amazing act of bravery on a daily basis but see the majority of their produce shipped to Spain, France or even further afield. I found it very humbling to be out on Kenny's boat at the mercy of the elements. I must have looked like a typical tourist and I'm sure the hardy divers had a good laugh at my expense. The chilled Scottish waters were actually warmer than the air outside and seeing scallops, crabs and lobsters in their natural habitat was thrilling. Just for the record I managed to relieve the ocean bed of 75 scallops (with a little help from my friends).

If consumers could request our native fish in shops and supermarkets this exporting of our national treasures would end. Although we are a tiny island surrounded by some of the most abundant waters in the northern hemisphere, over 80% of all the fish that is caught in our waters gets shipped abroad, whilst we import, more fashionable, but often lesser-quality fish from the other side of the world.

So be adventurous and make friends with your local fishmonger or buy directly from the fisherman and start requesting our native fish. There really is more to British fish than a fillet of cod.

Buying Fish

Choosing the best and freshest fish isn't as difficult as some people think. Very fresh fish should not smell fishy; it should just have a faint aroma of the sea. The eyes should be clear and bright, not dull and cloudy and they should protrude slightly from the head. Probably the most important place to check is the gills. They should be bright rosy red, with no hint of brown, and shouldn't be covered in a gooey film of mucus.

It's always best to buy whole fish, even if you need fillets. You can ask your fishmonger to fillet the fish for you, then you can take the bones and trimmings home and make fish stock with them. If you have to buy ready filleted, avoid soggy or discoloured fillets. They may have been frozen and will never have the flavour of really fresh fish. If you can't get the fish you want, a good strategy is to buy the best-looking fish in the shop and adapt your recipe to suit. An experienced fishmonger will be able to advise you on this. Buy on the day that you want to eat it – certainly no more than 24 hours in advance, then take it straight home and refrigerate as soon as possible.

This dish was inspired by Heston Blumenthal's white chocolate with caviar, and you'll be surprised how well the combination works. If you have time, do bury a whole truffle in the uncooked rice for about 3 days beforehand so that the rice absorbs the aroma. In other recipes I've used a basic risotto recipe (see page 209), but for this recipe it really does benefit the dish if you cook the rice with the chopped truffle in.

White Chocolate and White Truffle Risotto with Pan-fried Scallops

SERVES 4
20 g white truffle
75 g finely chopped shallots
25 g butter
150 g carnaroli or arborio
   risotto rice
100 ml white wine
1 litre of white chicken stock
   (see page 199), reserving 100 ml
2 tablespoons white truffle oil
2 tablespoons mascarpone
100 g Parmesan cheese
1 lemon for juice
50 g white chocolate buttons
8 cleaned and trimmed scallops,
   cut in half widthways
30 nasturtium leaves, to garnish
salt

USE A SMALL pairing knife to peel the truffle. Dice half of the truffle and leave the remainder whole.

IN A WARM, covered pan slowly sweat the shallots and the trimmings from the truffle for 2–3 minutes without letting them colour. Add the risotto rice and stir in thoroughly. Sweat for a further minute, again without letting the ingredients colour.

ADD THE WHITE wine and turn up the heat slightly. Stir continuously until the white wine has been absorbed by the rice. Start to add the stock, 100 ml at a time, stirring continuously. When all the stock has been absorbed taste a small spoonful of rice (it should be slightly undercooked so you can reheat it later). Season the risotto with salt, then pour the rice onto a large tray and spread it out evenly, which will stop the cooking process more quickly than leaving it in the pan. Cover with greaseproof paper to stop the rice drying out.

HEAT THE RESERVED 100 ml stock in a pan and add the cooked rice, gently stirring it in with a wooden spoon. Add the diced truffle and the truffle oil, then add the mascarpone cheese, 50 g grated Parmesan, the lemon juice and, finally, the white chocolate. At this stage you may need to adjust the seasoning to your taste. The salt and the Parmesan obviously give a savoury, salty background, the mascarpone adds a layer of creaminess, the lemon juice adds freshness to the rich flavours and the white chocolate, which is added right at the end, gives you surprising sweetness, and whether you add more of each ingredient is entirely up to you, bearing in mind that the scallops will be sweet, the nasturtium will be peppery and the shaved Parmesan salty.

SEASON THE SCALLOPS and fry them, cut side down, in a large, nonstick frying pan until they are become golden brown. Turn them over and cook for a further minute. Add a dash of lemon juice and lay them on a piece of kitchen paper.

TO SERVE, spoon the risotto on to the plates and place the fried scallops on top. Shave the remaining Parmesan and truffle and scatter over the top. Garnish with nasturtium leaves.

In the scallop recipes in this book I suggest that you keep the skirts and rinse and freeze them for later use. Here is one of those uses – scallop tripe. The dish would be fine without it, but I could eat it by the plateful. Do buy good quality hand-dived scallops in their shells. These are the only scallops that will absorb the red wine. Often scallops are soaked in water, making them expand (and increasing their weight) so they cannot absorb the marinade.

Scallops Poached in Red Wine with Scallop Tripe and Avocado

SERVES 4
4 extra large hand-dived scallops
1 bottle of red wine, such as a
    Bordeaux
10 sprigs of thyme
500 ml white chicken stock
    (see page 199)
1 Morteaux sausage or good quality
    smoked sausage (about 250 g)
2 large, ripe avocados
lemon juice
vegetable oil
1/2 quantity red wine sauce
    (see page 211)
1 quantity scallop tripe
    (see page 86)
salt

ASK YOUR FISHMONGER to open and clean the scallops for you. (Try to make sure that he does not leave them in water for too long.) Put the cleaned scallop meat into half of the red wine and add half the thyme sprigs. Make sure that the scallops are fully immersed in the wine and leave to marinade for 24 hours.

PUT THE REMAINDER of the wine in a small, deep saucepan with the rest of the thyme. Heat and hold the temperature at no more than 60°C/140°F (use an electric thermometer to help you).

PUT THE STOCK in a large saucepan, bring to the boil, add the sausage, simmer for 10 minutes and then allow the sausage to cool in the poaching liquor. When it is cool, peel away the skin away from the sausage and slice finely. Set aside eight slices (the remainder can be frozen for use later). Keep warm.

PEEL THE AVOCADOS and cut thick (1 cm) slices from the sides. Use a pastry cutter that has the same diameter as your scallops to cut out four discs from the flesh. Coat them with lemon juice (to prevent oxidization) and set aside. Put the remaining avocado flesh into a blender and blend until smooth. Season with lemon juice and salt and pass through a fine sieve. Set aside.

PUT THE SCALLOPS into the warm red wine and poach for at least 12 minutes. The scallops should feel firm once cooked.

MEANWHILE, heat a little vegetable oil in a small, ovenproof, nonstick frying pan, season the avocado discs with salt and roast them in a preheated oven at 180°C/350°F/gas 4 until soft and golden brown. In a separate saucepan heat the red wine sauce and the scallop tripe.

TO SERVE, place a spoonful of avocado purée in the centre of each plates, sit the roasted avocado disc on top of the purée and spoon the red wine sauce around the purée. Sit one slice of sausage on the avocado, then the scallop tripe and then another slice of sausage. Remove the scallop from the red wine and slice the top off it to expose the white meat inside. Sit it on top of the sausage.

The red pepper crumb in this recipe can be stored and used for a number of different dishes, and you'll even find it in a dessert with strawberries (see page 184). Before attempting this recipe make sure you have enough time to prepare the red pepper crumbs. Ask your fishmonger to fillet and skin the John Dory for you.

John Dory with Red Pepper Crumb and Chorizo Risotto

SERVES 4
2 red peppers
1 small chorizo sausage
300 ml white chicken stock
  (see page 199)
1 quantity risotto base
  (see page 209)
2 John Dory, skinned and filleted
50 g butter, diced
juice of 1 lemon
1 quantity red pepper crumbs
  (see page 214)
1 teaspoon diced rosemary leaves
1 tablespoon smoked paprika
50 g crème fraîche
25 g Parmesan cheese, grated
salt and pepper
basil, nasturtium or buckler sorrel
  leaves, to garnish

HOLD THE RED PEPPERS over an open flame and char the skin. Put the peppers into a freezer bag and allow to sweat for 5 minutes or until the skin can be easily removed. Core and deseed the pepper, cut the flesh into fine dice and set aside.

CUT THE CHORIZO into 1 cm dice and dry-fry in a casserole pan. Add the red pepper dice and the stock and allow to infuse for 15–20 minutes. Add the risotto rice and stir gently.

SEASON THE JOHN DORY fillets and dry-fry in a hot nonstick pan. This should take about 2 minutes in all: cook for 1½ minutes on one side to caramelize, turn over, add the butter and cook for a further 30 seconds on the other side. Season the fish with a dash of lemon juice and immediately put them in the red pepper crumbs. Roll the fish in the crumbs so that they are totally coated.

FINISH THE RISOTTO by adding the chopped rosemary, smoked paprika, crème fraîche and the grated Parmesan. Season with a little lemon juice and salt if needed.

TO SERVE, spoon the risotto into four large bowls, place the fish on top and dress with some basil, nasturtium or buckler sorrel.

Use the head (thicker end) of the cod fillet for this recipe because it will hold together, like a nice steak, and use a temperature probe to check if it's cooked in the middle. You can serve this fish with a sorrel and nasturtium salad and some tomato confit (see page 210) or some roasted baby artichokes.

Baked Cod with Red Pepper Crust and Aubergine Confit

SERVES 4
2 large aubergines
4 banana shallots, peeled
3 garlic cloves, peeled
250 ml olive oil
4 sprigs of thyme
10 basil leaves, torn
4 boneless, skinless cod fillets,
    140 g each
1 quantity red pepper crust
    (see page 214)
100 ml fish stock (see page 200)
salt and pepper

PEEL THE AUBERGINES, cut off the head end and chop the flesh into 3 cm dice. Cut the shallots into 3 cm piece and halve the garlic cloves. In a large, hot, ovenproof frying pan heat the olive oil. Carefully add the aubergines, shallots, garlic and thyme. Season with salt and pepper and stir to mix thoroughly. Cook in a preheated oven at 160°C/310°F/gas 2½ for about 20 minutes. When the aubergines are cooked, drain them in a colander, catching the oil underneath in a bowl. Put the aubergines on a chopping board and chop with a large knife, transfer to a bowl and mix in the torn basil leaves. Check the seasoning and set aside.

LAY THE COD on the red pepper crust and cut around the fish; the crust should be the same size as the pieces of cod. Spoon the fish stock and a dash of olive oil onto a nonstick baking tray. Place the cod fillets on the tray so that they are what would have been skin side up and season with salt and pepper. Spoon the aubergine confit over the fish so that the surface of the fish is completely covered. Place the pieces of pepper crust on top of the aubergines and put all four pieces of cod under a preheated hot grill. The crust will begin to mould itself around the aubergines almost immediately, and then it will begin to caramelize. When this happens, cook in a preheated oven at 180°C/350°F/gas 4 for at least 6 minutes (depending on the thickness of the cod). Then simply serve with the garnish of your choice.

I'm not really a fan of using dried beans. I'd rather wait until the fresh ones come into season. You will be able to find fresh borlotti beans in a good Italian delicatessen. Ask your fishmonger to de-scale the cod before cutting it into steaks.

Cod with Borlotti Beans and Vanilla

SERVES 4
4 boneless cod steaks, 120 g each
1 kg fresh Borlotti beans
1 onion, peeled
1 carrot, peeled
150 g smoked bacon
3 garlic cloves
6 large sprigs of thyme
500 g silver skin button onions
100 g butter
1 teaspoon caster sugar
100 ml white chicken stock
   (see page 199)
2 vanilla pods
4 large sprigs of tarragon, chopped
juice of 1 lemon
olive oil
8 braised and deboned chicken
   wings (as in the recipe on
   page 102)
50 ml brown chicken stock
   (see page 199)
12 pennywort salad leaves
salt

SHELL THE BEANS, put them in a large casserole pan, cover with cold water and bring to the boil. Drain away the water and cover again with fresh cold water. Cut the carrot and onion in half lengthways and add them to the water with the beans with the smoked bacon, the garlic and the thyme. Bring to the boil and simmer for about 2 hours. When the beans are cooked add a good handful of salt and allow to cool. (For some reason, if you add the salt to your beans or pulses before cooking, it stops the skin from softening.)

MEANWHILE, PEEL the baby onions, taking care to leave the root of the onion intact to help prevent the onions from falling apart. Put them in a pan with 25 g butter, a little salt, the sugar and the rest of the thyme sprigs. Cook to caramelize slightly, drain away the butter and add the stock. Cover and cook for 15 minutes. The chicken stock will have reduced and you will have a shiny, sweet emulsion. Set aside and keep warm.

REMOVE THE VEGETABLES, thyme and smoked bacon from the beans. Drain the beans, reserving the liquid, and return them to the same pan. Add 250 ml of the reserved cooking liquid, scrape in the seeds from the vanilla pods and reduce until almost dry. While the pan is still on a very low heat gradually add 50 g butter, stirring gently with a wooden spoon. The butter and the stock will eventually emulsify. Add the onions and the tarragon. Season with salt, if needed, and half the lemon juice.

SEASON THE COD with salt and put it, skin side down, in a hot nonstick frying pan with a little olive oil. Cook over a fairly high heat for about 2 minutes until the skin is crispy. Turn over and cook for a further 2–3 minutes. Add the remaining butter and cook for a further minute. Season with the remaining lemon juice and remove to a warm plate.

REHEAT THE CHICKEN wings in the chicken jus.

SPOON THE BEANS into four large bowls and arrange the cod on top. Put the chicken wings on the plates and garnish with pennywort.

A good crayfish reaches maturity at about five years old, and it's best to stay away from them during the winter months because they mate in September or October and then hatch in early summer. I think that peas go fantastically well with crayfish, and both are at their peak at the same time. I'm also a great fan of pairing meat and shellfish, especially something as delicate as rabbit and crayfish.

Crayfish with Rabbit and Peas

SERVES 4
2 whole rabbits
500 ml duck fat
butter, melted
8 slices of pancetta
200 g pork or veal mince
½ quantity shallot confit
   (see page 210)
1 tablespoon chopped tarragon
   leaves
200 ml crayfish stock
   (see page 200)
50 ml cream
4 gelatine leaves, softened
2 tablespoons crème fraîche
4 leaves of mint, finely shredded
1 kg fresh peas in their pods
juice and rind of 1 lemon
1 kg freshwater crayfish
200 g frozen peas
pea shoots and pea flowers to dress
sugar
salt and ground white pepper

The freshest crayfish are alive and frisky. To check, stay well out of their claw range, grasp them firmly by the sides and hold them upside down. Live ones will wriggle. Put live crayfish in a bowl, cover with a damp kitchen paper and keep refrigerated for no more the 24 hours. Fresh crayfish are best cooked and eaten on the same day, but they can be safely kept for up to 2 days in the refrigerator after being cooked.

REMOVE THE HIND and front legs from the rabbit. Put the front legs in a large casserole dish with the duck fat and cook over as low a heat as possible for at least 2 hours. Meanwhile, remove the bones from the hind legs, keeping the meat intact. Lay the leg meat between two sheets of clingfilm and use a meat mallet (or the base of a fairly heavy pan) to flatten the meat. Lay a large sheet of foil on your work surface, brush it butter and lay out the pancetta to form rectangle with one of the long sides nearest you. Lay the flattened rabbit legs, skin side down, over the bacon and season with salt and pepper.

MIX THE MINCE with the shallot confit, tarragon leaves and plenty of seasoning. Spoon the mixture over the flattened legs, spreading it horizontally from end to end. Using the foil to help and beginning with the side nearest you, roll the bacon and rabbit into a large sausage shape (ballotine). Fasten the ends of the foil as tightly as possible and immerse the ballotine in the warm duck fat. Cook for at least 2 hours (remove the front legs when they have been in the fat for 2 hours). When it is cooked, take it from the fat, remove the foil and rewrap in clingfilm to help reform the shape that may have been lost during cooking. Transfer to the refrigerator until it is fully chilled, then cut the ballotine into four slices 3 cm thick. Place them on a wire rack and keep them in the refrigerator.

DIVIDE THE STOCK into two batches and put them in two separate saucepans. Add the cream to one saucepan. Heat them both, reducing the one with the cream by a third. Put one of the softened gelatine leaves in each and stir to dissolve. Pass them both separately through a fine sieve and allow to set slightly. Spoon the creamed stock over the ballotine slices and allow to set, then spoon over the dark stock and again allow to set. When they are both set use a small knife to scrape away the set stocks from the sides, exposing the bacon. Keep the slices refrigerated until you need them.

PICK THE MEAT from the front legs. Put it in a small bowl and mix in the crème fraîche and mint. Set aside.

SHELL THE PEAS and blanch them in plenty of boiling salted water until they are soft, then refresh them in iced water. Drain and gently crush half of the peas and mix them with the front leg meat. Season with a little salt and the grated lemon rind.

REMOVE THE TAILS from the crayfish, blanch them briefly in boiling water and refresh in iced water. Remove the tails from the shells and set aside.

REMOVE THE LOIN from the rabbit and trim away all the sinew. Remove the rack from the rabbit and prepare it as if you were preparing a French trimmed rack of lamb, although on a smaller scale.

BLANCH THE FROZEN PEAS in boiling salted water, then blend until smooth in a blender. Add the remaining gelatine while the mixture is still in the blender, then pass the pea purée through a fine sieve and season with salt and a little sugar if needed. Line a flat tray with clingfilm and brush it lightly with olive oil. Spoon a couple of tablespoons onto the tray, spreading it out into a rectangle 7 x 5 cm. Repeat to make four rectangles. Transfer to the refrigerator for an hour or two to set, then spoon the front leg meat mixture in the middle purée and use the clingfilm to help you roll it into a cannelloni shape. Keep in the refrigerator until required.

HEAT A FRYING PAN. Season the rabbit loin and rack with salt and pepper, add a dash of oil to the pan, add the loin and rack and caramelize on all sides. About 30 seconds before you remove the meat from the pan add the seasoned crayfish tails and caramelize. Season all this with a little lemon juice and remove from the pan.

SLICE THE LOINS in half lengthways, put them on four plates and sit the chilled pea cannelloni on top. Sit the ballotines next to the loins, cut the rack into cutlets and arrange these on the plates with the crayfish tails. Dress the remaining peas and pea shoots with a dash of lemon juice and olive oil and a pinch of salt and arrange them over the racks.

The stuffing for this Dover sole dish would also sit comfortably under the skin of a chicken for your Sunday roast. Ask your fishmonger to cut away the heads of the fish and to skin them and trim off the skirts. I would serve this with green beans and a foie gras ravioli (see page 25).

Dover Sole with Artichokes, Potato, Foie Gras and Chicken Liver

SERVES 4
2 Dover soles, 600 g each
2 large globe artichokes
juice of 1 lemon
1 large chipping potato
150 g very fresh chicken livers
150 g foie gras
25 ml olive oil
75 g butter, diced
1 tablespoon thyme leaves
2 tablespoons chopped flat
  leaf parsley
50 ml balsamic vinegar
salt and pepper

RUN A SHARP KNIFE down the backbone of the sole on both sides and cut out the backbone. You should now have two pieces of fish with the bone left in the centre.

PEEL AWAY THE LEAVES from the globe artichokes and snapping off the stalks. Trim all the green away from the hearts and scoop out the chokes from the centre. Put them straight into water with some lemon juice to stop them from oxidizing. Dice the artichoke as finely and as evenly as possible and keep it in the water. Cut the potato into dice the same size as the artichoke and keep the pieces in cold water.

DICE THE CHICKEN livers as finely as possible and put them on clean kitchen paper.

FINELY DICE the foie gras. You will find it easier if you partially freeze the foie gras before trying to dice it and keep dipping your knife into a jug of very hot water. Keep the foie gras and the chicken livers in the refrigerator until you need them.

SEASON AND PAN-FRY the fish fillets in a large, hot, nonstick frying pan for about 5 minutes until they are golden brown on both sides. Take the fillets off the bone and set aside. Keep the top and bottom of each fillet together.

DRAIN THE LIQUID from the artichokes and potatoes and dry on kitchen paper. Put the olive oil in a hot nonstick frying pan, add a couple of knobs of butter, add the drained artichoke and potato dice and season with salt and pepper. Fry until golden brown, then add the diced foie gras and chicken livers. Cook for a further minute and then add the picked thyme leaves, the flat leaf parsley and the balsamic vinegar. Stir and then remove immediately from the heat and drain onto a clean tea towel.

LAY THE FOUR bottom fillets of Dover sole on a nonstick baking tray, season with a little salt and then spoon foie gras and chicken liver mixture onto the fillets. Put the remaining fillets on top and reheat in the hot oven for a couple of minutes. Transfer to plates and serve.

When buying skate, do ask your fishmonger to skin the skate wings for you because their thorns can be extremely sharp. In the old days skate used to paired with strong flavours because, if it isn't stored on ice as soon as it comes out of the water, it starts to give off a strong odour of ammonia – a clear sign of poor handling.

Roasted Skate with Poached Egg, Parsley Sauce and Capers

SERVES 4
2 large potatoes
4 large, very red plum tomatoes
250 ml fish stock (see page 200)
100 g butter
1 quantity parsley purée
  (see page 139, step four)
4 eggs
25 g capers
2 tablespoons chopped flat
  leaf parsley
4 skate wings, skinned, 1 kg each

CUT THE POTATOES into 1 cm dice and keep in cold water. Blanch the tomatoes for 10 seconds in salted water, plunge them immediately into iced water and peel their skins away. Don't leave the tomatoes in the water for too long or they will absorb the water. Cut each tomato into four. Remove the seeds and cut the flesh into dice the same size as the potato.

HEAT THE FISH stock and reduce it by half. Whisk in one-third of the butter. Add the parsley purée, season with a little salt and set aside.

POACH THE EGGS and keep them warm.

YOU WILL PROBABLY need two large frying pans for this recipe. Heat one of them and some olive oil. Drain the potato and dry on a tea towel. Add a third of the butter to the pan with the oil, add the dry potatoes and caramelize. When the potatoes are cooked and coloured add the capers, the diced tomato and the chopped parsley.

HEAT THE OTHER frying pan and add enough olive oil to cover the bottom. Season the thicker side of the skate wing and place this, seasoned side down, in the frying pan, taking care that you do not splash yourself with hot oil. Cook the fish for 4 minutes on the seasoned side and then remove from the pan. Transfer to a chopping board, caramelized side up, and insert a knife into the thicker part of the fish, against the bone. Run your knife all the way to the thinner end, removing the flesh from the bone.

PUT THE WARM POTATO mixture in the centre of the plates, spoon the parsley sauce around. Place the boneless skate wing on top of the garnish with a poached egg on top.

You can prepare a lot of this dish in advance. The only thing that needs to be done at the last minute is popping the fish into the steamer so you can sit down and enjoy your evening. In Britain the wild sea trout season opens on 15 March and closes on 30 September, but the fish are at their best from May to July time. The British crab season runs from May to October, making this dish a perfect partnership as far as the key ingredients are concerned.

Sea Trout with Crab and Ginger Mousse, wrapped in Lettuce with Carrot and Lemon Grass Sauce

SERVES 4
25 g fresh ginger, peeled
150 g picked white crabmeat
100 g chicken mousse
   (see page 214)
10 coriander leaves, finely
   shredded
finely grated rind of 1 lemon
2 round butterhead lettuce
4 portions of boneless, skinless
   wild sea trout, 120 g each
6 stalks of lemon grass
300 g new season carrots, peeled
   and finely sliced
75 g butter, diced
2 star anise
1 litre of white chicken stock
   (see page 199)
200 ml double cream
juice of 1 lemon
salt and pepper
coriander leaves, to garnish

DICE THE GINGER as finely as possible, place in a small saucepan, cover with cold salted water and bring to the boil. Drain and repeat the process about six times until the ginger is soft. Dry on kitchen paper.

PICK THROUGH the white crabmeat to make sure there is no cartilage or shell, and dry on kitchen paper. Transfer to a large bowl and add the chicken mousse and coriander leaves and ginger. Season with salt, pepper and lemon rind, cover with clingfilm and leave in the refrigerator for a couple of hours.

SELECT THE BEST LEAVES from the lettuce. Have a large bowl of iced water ready. Bring a large saucepan of water to the boil, 1 tablespoon of salt and plunge the lettuce leaves in for a few seconds. Remove with a slotted spoon and quickly place into the iced water. The lettuce leaves will be wilted, but still hold a crunch and be bright green. Once they are cold, drain them of any water and lay them out on kitchen paper to dry.

ON A SHEET OF CLINGFILM lay two large lettuce leaves end to end to create one large leaf. Sit a piece of fish in the centre of each 'leaf' and spoon a quarter of the mousse on top of the fish. Add the softened ginger. Fold over the lettuce to create a parcel, using the clingfilm to get a tight seal. Repeat to make four parcels and chill until you are ready.

MAKE THE CARROT purée. Bruise the lemongrass with the back of a chopping knife. The more you bruise it the more flavour you extract. Chop into small pieces. In a large, warm, covered pan sweat the carrots with the butter, lemon grass and star anise for 10–15 minutes without letting them colour. When the carrots are soft add the stock, reduce by half, add the cream and again reduce by half. Transfer to a blender and blend until smooth. Pass through a fine sieve twice. Season with salt, lemon juice and sugar, if necessary.

PLACE THE FISH in the steamer and cook for 6–7 minutes, then leave to sit for a further minute.

TO SERVE, reheat the carrot purée and spoon onto each plate. Cut each piece of fish in half widthways and arrange on top of the carrot purée. Dress each dish with some coriander leaves.

Summer, summer, summer. As soon as summer arrives, this dish goes onto the lunch menu in the restaurant and it's a dish I will cook when friends and family come for dinner. It's a fairly easy dish to prepare and it screams freshness.

Halibut with Beetroot and Orange Salad

SERVES 4
1 large beetroot
1 large fennel bulb
4 boneless halibut steaks,
   130 g each
20 g butter
juice of 1 lemon
olive oil
leaves of 4 large sprigs of tarragon,
   chopped
4 blood oranges, divided into
   segments
100 g beetroot purée
   (see page 204)
½ quantity orange vinaigrette
   (see page 211)

WRAP THE BEETROOT in foil and bake it in a preheated oven at 160°C/310°F/gas 2½ for 1 hour. When it is cool peel away the skin and cut the flesh into 5 mm dice. Set aside.

SLICE THE FENNEL lengthways on a mandolin as thin as you can.

SEASON THE HALIBUT and fry it in a large, very hot nonstick pan until golden brown on both sides. Treat the halibut as if you were cooking a steak, constantly turning the fish until it is cooked to your liking. When it has reached your desired cooking temperature add a knob of butter and cook for a further 30 seconds. Add a dash of lemon juice and remove to a warm plate.

DRESS THE FENNEL slices with a little olive oil, some lemon juice and a sprinkle of salt and add the tarragon and orange segments.

SMEAR A SPOONFUL of beetroot purée on the plate, place a pile of the diced beetroot in the centre with the halibut on top. Pile some fennel salad next to the fish and drizzle with orange vinaigrette.

Poaching fish is a delicate process. Getting the timing and the temperature right is essential so, if you haven't already got one, I suggest you buy an electric thermometer. When you're buying a luxurious flat fish such as turbot or brill, always try and buy fillets from a larger fish, such as a 4 kg fish. I'm sure if you ask your fishmonger well in advance he will be happy to get it for you. The flavour and texture are worth it.

Poached Turbot with Truffle Cream, Chervil and Mushrooms

SERVES 4
1 litre fish stock (see page 200)
6 large sprigs of thyme
75 g button mushrooms
4 large shallots, thinly sliced
100 g butter, diced
1 bay leaf
100 ml Madeira
juice of 1 lemon
200 g chervil, plus extra for garnishing
4 portions of boneless, skinless turbot, 125 g each
50 g truffle cream sauce, warmed (see page 212)
3 large scallops
16 slices of truffled potato (see page 140)
salt and pepper
2 garlic cloves, thinly sliced

SCALLOP TRIPE (OPTIONAL)
1 carrot
1/2 head of garlic
3 shallots
50 g smoked bacon
25 g butter
6 large sprigs of thyme
2 bay leaves
scallop skirts
250 ml red wine
100 ml port
250 ml brown chicken stock (see page 199)
salt

IF YOU'VE DECIDED to make the scallop tripe allow 3–4 hours cooking time. Chop the carrot, garlic, shallots and bacon into pieces that are roughly the same size. Caramelize them in a hot casserole with the butter and a little salt. When they are golden brown add the thyme and bay leaves and cook for a further minute. Drain the butter away and add the drained scallop skirts, add the red wine and port and cook to reduce by two-thirds. The scallop skirts will begin to absorb the red wine and port and take on a deep red colour. Add the stock, bring back to the boil, cover with a tight-fitting lid and cook in a preheated oven at 140°C/275°F/gas 1 for 2–2½ hours.

WHEN THE SKIRTS are cooked you will be able to eat them without them being chewy. Drain the cooking liquor through a colander and set aside. Separate the skirts from the vegetables and set aside. Reduce the cooking liquor by a third and bind this back into the skirts and keep warm. (You can freeze this to use later.)

PUT THE FISH STOCK in a flat-bottomed pan over a low heat. Season with half the thyme leaves. Insert your electric thermometer and set the maximum temperature at 60°C/140°F.

FINELY CHOP THE MUSHROOMS in a food processor. In a warm pan sweat the shallots with the butter, bay leaf and thyme sprigs until soft, add the chopped button mushrooms and cook, without a lid, for 15–20 minutes, stirring occasionally. Once the mushrooms have turned into a dark, dry paste, add the Madeira and reduce until dry. Season the mushroom now salt and a little lemon juice. Keep this mushroom duxelle warm.

PICK 12 SPRIGS of chervil for garnishing later. Chop the rest finely.

MAKE SURE YOU have a bowl of iced water with another stainless steel bowl sitting inside it. Boil the remaining stock and cream together, reduce by half, add two-thirds of the chopped chervil and reboil. Immediately pour the mixture into the blender and blend until smooth and green. Halfway way through blending add the remaining chopped chervil. When the sauce is smooth pass through the sieve

into the chilled stainless steel bowl. Stir until the sauce becomes cold. Add a little salt if necessary.

SEASON THE TURBOT with salt and pepper and immerse in the fish stock, which should now be exactly 60°C/140°F. Cook for 12–13 minutes. When the turbot is cooked remove it from the stock and put it in the warm truffle cream.

FINALLY, SLICE the scallops into wafer-thin slices. You need 12 slices in all. Season them with a drop of olive oil, a little lemon juice, sea salt and a sprinkling of chopped chervil.

REHEAT THE TRUFFLED potato slices in the steamer and arrange them on four plates. Spoon three piles of mushroom duxelle onto each plates and cover each with a scallop slice. Spoon the scallop tripe onto the plate, spoon the chervil sauce around and place the fish on top of the tripe. Garnish with chervil.

This is a play on the classic dish Devils on Horseback. I also like to serve this as a garnish with Dover sole, and it even works well with beef fillet and watercress salad. I've tried many oysters in my career, and those from Carlingford in Northern Ireland stand head and shoulders above them all.

Carlingford Oysters Wrapped in Smoked Bacon with Avocado Purée and Red Wine Sauce

SERVES 4
12 large rock oysters, opened
   (see below)
8 wafer-thin slices of smoked
   pancetta
3 large, ripe Haas avocados
juice of 1 lemon
olive oil
½ teaspoon vitamin C powder
250 ml red wine sauce
   (see page 211)
25 g butter
salt

WRAP EIGHT OF THE OYSTERS in the smoked pancetta and set aside.

PEEL THE AVOCADOS and slice the flesh of one of them on a mandolin. Transfer the slices to a sheet of greaseproof paper and dress with lemon juice and olive oil to stop them from oxidizing. Chop the remaining avocados and place the flesh in a blender. Add the remaining lemon juice, the vitamin C powder and a little salt. Blend until smooth, pass through a fine sieve and store in a container in the refrigerator with a sheet of clingfilm pushed firmly down onto the purée.

REDUCE THE RED WINE sauce by half, add the butter and whisk in until emulsified.

HEAT SOME OLIVE OIL in nonstick frying pan gently sear the wrapped oysters on all sides. Roll the remaining four oysters in the avocado slices.

DRESS FOUR PLATES with the purée, sit the roasted oysters and the avocado-wrapped oysters on the purée and dress with the red wine sauce.

Oysters are a delicate ingredient and should preferably be kept closed until the last minute, so that all the juices and freshness stay within the shells. Wrap them in damp kitchen paper and store them in the refrigerator. Do not store live oysters in airtight containers or they will die. They will keep in their shells for 2–3 days; always ask your fishmonger for their harvest date. If the shell is tightly closed the oyster is still alive. If the shell is slightly open, it should close promptly when tapped. If it does not throw it out. Don't take any risks.

Chill the oysters in the freezer for an hour or so to make them easier to open. When you remove the oysters from the freezer, allow them to rest for a few minutes before inserting an oyster knife between the top and bottom shell. Use a towel to protect your hand. Twist the knife to pry the halves apart. Work the knife around to the hinge muscle and cut through it. Do this over a bowl to catch the juices. Holding the deeper shell downwards, slide the knife between the oyster and the top shell. Detach the oyster. Slip the knife under the oyster and remove it from the bottom shell. Strain the juice from the shell and remove any bits of shell. Store the oysters in the strained liquid in the refrigerator until needed.

This potato 'risotto' garnish would also work beautifully with a piece of beef fillet. Roasted garlic is a good addition to the dish, but bear in mind that the garlic needs to be prepared in advance.

Roasted Turbot with New Potato and Blue Cheese Risotto and Red Wine Sauce

SERVES 4
1.5 kg Jersey Royal potatoes (or other waxy potatoes)
200 g butter
175 g blue cheese
50 g crème fraîche
2 tablespoons chopped flat leaf parsley
250 ml red wine sauce (see page 211)
4 boneless, skinless turbot steaks, 130 g each
100 g butter
juice of 1 lemon
4 heads of garlic
300 g duck fat
100 g honey
4 large sprigs of thyme
salt and pepper

PEEL THE POTATOES and cut them into 5 mm dice, making sure that they are the same size so that they cook at the same rate. It's best for the risotto if you don't keep your potatoes in water because they will loose a lot of the starch that you need.

CUT EACH HEAD of garlic in half and place the bottom halves in a roasting pan. Cover with duck fat and place in a preheated oven, 180°C/350°F/gas 4, for 2 hours, until the garlic is soft. Remove from the fat and place in a frying pan, cut side down. Add the honey and thyme and cook over a low heat until the garlic is caramelized. Keep warm.

MELT THE BUTTER in a nonstick pan and add the potatoes, season with salt and pepper and cook it fairly slowly. Don't let the potatoes colour. As you are cooking the potato it will begin to give of its starch and start sticking together. Turn the heat down slightly and keep stirring. There is no need to add stock because the potatoes will gradually give up their own liquid. Once the potatoes are cooked fold in the blue cheese, crème fraîche and chopped parsley.

REHEAT the red wine sauce.

SEASON THE TURBOT with salt and pepper and fry in a hot, nonstick frying pan for about 2–3 minutes, skin side down. Turn over the fish and cook for a further minute. Add the butter, cook for a further minute and sprinkle with a dash of lemon juice.

SERVE THE POTATO risotto on warm plates, add the fish and the garlic and pour the red wine sauce around.

This dish delivers a strong combination of flavours, and the garnishes can be used for a number of different dishes.

Roasted Monkfish with Pickled Yellow Peppers, Black Olives and Mussels

SERVES 4
4 small baby monkfish tails
   (bones in), 300–400 g each
1.5 kg pitted black olives
200 ml olive oil
100 g picked flat leaf parsley leaves
1 teaspoon thyme leaves
4 garlic cloves
100 g breadcrumbs
16–20 medium sized mussels
50 g plain flour
2 eggs, beaten
3 yellow peppers
6 large shallots
100 ml olive oil
50 g sugar
100 ml white wine vinegar
basil cress, to garnish
salt

USE A SHARP, thin knife to remove the skin and brown membranes from the outside of the monkfish.

SET THE OVEN to its lowest setting and cook the olives overnight. In the morning the olives should be like little black pellets. Put two-thirds of the olives in a blender with the olive oil and blend until the oil is black (this will take quite a few minutes). Pass the oil through a very fine sieve and set aside.

PLACE THE PARSLEY, thyme leaves, half of the garlic and all the breadcrumbs in a food processor and blend until the crumbs become totally green. Season with a little salt and set aside.

COOK AND PREPARE the mussels as on page 148. When the mussels are cold, remove them from the shells and toss them in the flour, coat in beaten egg and then cover in the green breadcrumbs.

HOLD THE YELLOW peppers over an open flame to char the skin. Put them straight into a freezer bag and close. After 5–10 minutes take the peppers out of the bag and peel away the skin. Core and deseed and finely shred the flesh.

PEEL AND FINELY slice the shallots and remaining garlic as finely as the yellow pepper. Put the garlic and shallot in a heavy-bottomed casserole pan and sweat them in olive oil without letting them colour. When they are soft add the thyme sprigs and yellow pepper, cook for a further 2 minutes and add the sugar. Cook for 2–3 minutes or until all the liquid from the sugar and peppers has evaporated. Add the white wine vinegar and reduce until dry. Season with salt.

COOK THE MONKFISH in a hot frying pan with olive oil. Depending on the thickness of the fish, you may need to cook them further in a hot oven, so use an ovenproof pan. When the fish is almost cooked, deep-fry the mussels until slightly crisp. Add the black olive oil to the fish and cook for a further 2 minutes, coating the fish in the black olive oil.

SPOON THE YELLOW pepper into the centre of the plate, carve the monkfish and dress with the deep-fried mussels and some basil cress.

I've been cooking this dish for years. The basil sauce is made from a crayfish stock and makes it so moreish. Buy your sea bass already scaled, filleted and pin-boned – unless you feel like having a go yourself. With this recipe it doesn't really matter what size fish you get your fillets from as long as they are big enough for one portion.

Sea Bass Stuffed with Crab, Basil Sauce and Watercress and Radish Salad

SERVES 4
4 portions of sea bass fillet
olive oil
300 g picked basil leaves
1 large mouli (daikon), peeled
 and thinly sliced
2 large bunches of picked
 watercress leaves
100 g picked white crabmeat
juice of 1 lemon
300 ml crayfish stock
 (see page 200)
100 g butter, diced
salt and pepper

ON YOUR WORK SURFACE lay out a sheet of clingfilm large enough to wrap a single fillet of sea bass. Brush it with a olive oil and lay a basil leaf on top, sprinkle with a little salt and pepper. Lay the sea bass fillet, skin side down, on the clingfilm and wrap it up to create an airtight envelope. Repeat with the other three fillets. Keep refrigerated until needed.

COOK THE REMAINING basil leaves in a very large pan of boiling, salted water for 3–4 minutes. Drain the water and place the basil in a blender and blend until smooth. You may need to add a little of the blanching water to help it blend. Pass through a very fine sieve into a chilled bowl and immediately transfer to the refrigerator to chill. (This is quite a messy job.)

CUT THE MOULI SLICES into long strips. Mix them in an ovenproof dish with the watercress leaves, the crabmeat, some olive oil, lemon juice and salt.

PLACE THE FISH PARCELS, still in the clingfilm and skin side down, in the steamer and steam for 5–7 minutes (the thicker the fillets, the longer they will take to cook).

ADD THE BUTTER to the crayfish stock and heat until reduced by half.

PUT THE DISH containing the mouli salad in a hot oven for a couple of minutes to allow the salad leaves to wilt slightly.

MEANWHILE, whisk the basil purée into the stock and season with a pinch of salt if needed. Pour the sauce into four bowls, divide the salad into four portions and place one in the middle of each bowl. Unwrap the fish, season with a little more salt and a dash of lemon juice and place on top of the salads.

This is one of the easiest dishes in this book. It is very rich in flavour, and it's essential to use really fresh fish. The squid ink sauce is optional. Your fishmonger will be able to get it for you if you ask in advance. It usually comes in 10 g packets, and it's worth getting some extra to keep in the freezer.

Red Mullet and Filo Tart with Black Olive and Basil

SERVES 4
4 filo tarts (see page 46, step one)
4 medium sized red mullet fillets, pin-boned
25 pitted black olives
2 garlic cloves
10 basil leaves
12 pickled anchovy fillets
olive oil
25 g Parmesan cheese, grated
10 g Parmesan cheese, finely shaved
150 ml fish stock (see page 200)
20 g squid ink
50 g butter, diced
juice of 1 lemon
2 punnets of baby basil

BEFORE YOU COOK the filo tarts, cut them out by cutting around a plate with a 14 cm circumference. Bake them as described on page 46.

WRAP THE FISH fillets in clingfilm, lay them flat, skin side down, and partially freeze them. This will make it easier to slice the flesh finely.

PUT THE OLIVES, garlic, basil leaves and four of the pickled anchovies into a food processor and blend until smooth. Add a little olive oil if the mix is too dry to blend.

SPREAD A THIN LAYER of the black olive paste onto the filo tarts and sprinkle over the grated Parmesan.

FINELY SLICE THE MULLET, making sure that you cut through the skin with each slice. Layer the red mullet onto the tarts and place two anchovy fillets on each tart. Scatter over the Parmesan shavings.

REDUCE THE FISH stock by two-thirds, add the squid ink and then stir in the butter. Season with a little lemon juice.

COOK THE TARTS under a preheated hot grill for no more than 2 minutes. Dress the plates with the squid ink sauce, place the tarts on top and scatter over the basil.

This is a simple recipe with complex flavours. I would use black bream, which is indigenous to British waters, even though the more common gilt head bream from the Mediterranean actually tastes rather better. The only real work involved in this dish is the lemon purée, which you can make well in advance. You can ask your fishmonger to skin and pin-bone the sea bream.

Sea Bream with Lemon Sauce, Crayfish and Sage Risotto

SERVES 4
500 ml white chicken stock
   (see page 199)
100 ml double cream
100 g lemon purée (see page 203)
1 kg fresh crayfish
1 lemon, cut into 8 slices
4 sea bream fillets (either silver
   or gilt head)
olive oil
1 quantity risotto base
   (see page 209)
10 sage leaves
rind of 1 lemon
2 tablespoons mascarpone cheese
50 g Parmesan cheese, grated
sprigs of fennel, to garnish
salt and pepper

MAKE THE LEMON SAUCE. Heat 400 ml of the chicken stock and reduce it by two-thirds, add the double cream and reduce by one-third again. Whisk in the lemon purée and check the seasoning. Cover the sauce with clingfilm and set aside.

PREPARE THE CRAYFISH as in the recipe on page 78.

LAY THE LEMON slices on a nonstick baking tray. Put the fish fillets on top of the lemon (two slices to each fillet). Brush the fish with a little olive oil and a small amount of the chicken stock to help keep it moist while cooking. Season each fillet with salt and pepper. Bake in a preheated oven at 160°C/310°F/gas 2½ for 10–12 minutes. Carefully place the cooked fillets on a wire rack with a plate underneath. Spoon the lemon sauce over the fish so that each fillet is completely coated.

HEAT THE REMAINING chicken stock and add the risotto base, sage leaves, lemon rind, mascarpone and Parmesan.

PAN FRY THE CRAYFISH in a hot frying pan with a little olive oil for only about 30 seconds to a minute.

SPOON THE RISOTTO onto four plates, place the fish on one side and the crayfish tails on the other side. Dress with some baby fennel and bronze fennel.

Meat

The combination of chicken and figs came about when one of my trusted suppliers, Steve Downey from Chef Direct in Bristol sent me through his daily price list and there was a chicken on there that was fed on a diet of figs. I think they cost as much as £14 each, but boy, are they worth it! If you're reading this book I'm assuming that you're a fairly keen cook and that I don't really have to advise you on what kind of chicken to buy.

Chicken Breast with Lemon, Rosemary and Figs

SERVES 4
1 litre white chicken stock
   (see page 199)
3 large sprigs of rosemary
rind of 1 lemon
1 large organic, free-range chicken,
   about 1.5 kg
1 quantity potato gnocchi
   (see page 205)
6 black figs
50 ml honey
200 ml double cream
4 large tablespoons lemon purée
   (see page 203)
juice of ½ lemon (optional)
100 ml brown chicken stock
   (see page 199)
buckler sorrel leaves, to garnish
salt and pepper

HEAT THE CHICKEN STOCK in a large ovenproof casserole and add two sprigs of rosemary and the lemon rind. Cut the legs and the backbone from the chicken, remove the wish bone, season generously with salt and pepper and add to the stock. Turn down the heat and simmer for 10–12 minutes. Remove the casserole from the heat and leave the chicken to cool down in the stock.

MEANWHILE, finely chop the remaining rosemary and use it to flavour the potato gnocchi.

CUT EACH FIG INTO FOUR SLICES, lie them on a tray and drizzle over the honey.

REMOVE THE CHICKEN from the stock and reduce the stock by two-thirds. Add the cream and reduce by half. Remove the rosemary and pass the mixture through a fine sieve. Transfer it to a blender and, while it is still warm, add the lemon purée and blend until smooth. You may need to adjust the seasoning with a little salt and sugar; it will taste a little fresher with the juice of half a lemon added. Set aside and keep warm.

TAKE THE CHICKEN BREAST from the bone. Remove the skin and slice the flesh thinly. Lay the slices on a plate and reheat in a steamer.

REHEAT THE BROWN CHICKEN STOCK. Quickly cook the chicken slices under the grill for 30 seconds or so and reheat the gnocchi in the lemon sauce.

ARRANGE ALL THE INGREDIENTS on four plates, spoon over the chicken jus over and garnish with some buckler sorrel.

This is one of those recipes that has evolved from a combination of dishes that I've cooked in various restaurants. The potato soup is a Tom Aikens classic. I've teamed it with some baked bread. All the ingredients are quite rich, but the bitterness of the raw sorrel really cuts through them. This is a perfect lunchtime dish: the ingredients complement each other really well.

Braised Chicken with Sourdough Bread and Potato Soup

SERVES 4
12 large, three-bone chicken
  wings, trimmed (see note below)
1 litre white chicken stock
  (see page 199)
4 large sprigs of thyme
1.5 litres semi-skimmed milk
500 g sourdough bread
100 g strong white bread flour
1 quantity mashed potato
  (see page 209)
25 ml white truffle oil
1 tablespoon finely shredded flat
  leaf parsley
150 g chicken liver parfait
  (see page 215)
sorrel salad leaves, to garnish
salt and pepper

For this (and other recipes in the book) you only need the centre joint of the wing. Remove the extra part with a sharp knife. You need to cut below the knuckle, leaving no knuckle on the wing, making it easier to remove the bone when the wing is cooked. Set the remaining chicken aside for making stock later.

PUT THE CENTRE JOINTS of the chicken wings in a saucepan, cover with water and bring to the boil. Allow to boil for a couple of minutes, then pour away the liquid. This will rid the wings of the scum and a good amount of the fat. Rinse the wings under cold running water for a couple of minutes, then put in a clean pan. Cover with stock, add the thyme, season with plenty of salt and cook over a low heat for about 2 hours or until the wings are soft and the two bones can be easily removed. Remove the wings from the stock. Before they cool completely remove the bones (it is much easier to do this while they are still warm). Put the wings in the refrigerator to chill. When they are chilled tidy the ends with a sharp knife, double-checking for any shattered bone.

REDUCE THE CHICKEN STOCK by half and set aside. Heat the milk in a large pan. Cut four slices of sourdough bread 1 cm thick, toast and keep warm. Slice the rest of the bread, put it on a baking tray in a preheated oven at 180°C/350°F/gas 4 and bake to the point just before burning.

PUT THE FLOUR IN A HOT FRYING PAN and cook, stirring, until the flour starts to colour and give off a smell reminiscent of baking. Add the baked bread trimmings and the cooked flour to 1 litre of the warm milk with 1 tablespoon of salt. Cover with a circle of greaseproof paper to prevent a skin forming and allow to sit for 1½ hours over a very low heat.

WHISK THE MASHED POTATO into the remaining warm milk, add the white truffle oil and correct the seasoning to your taste. Transfer to a gas canister, add a cartridge and shake well. Keep the canister warm in a pan of simmering water.

REHEAT THE CHICKEN WINGS in the reduced chicken stock and add the parsley. Strain the milk from the bread.

TO SERVE, put the warm chicken wings in the bottom of four soup bowls. Cover with the potato soup from the canister, then foam the bread milk as if you were making a cappuccino. Spread the chicken liver parfait on the toast and garnish with sorrel leaves.

This is a fairly simple starter or it can be used as a canapé. It is imperative that you source a large duck breast for this recipe and a good-quality soft goats' cheese.

Honey-smoked Duck with Truffled Goats' Cheese Mousse

SERVES 4
1 large Magret duck breast
100 ml honey
75 g wood chippings
150 g goats' cheese
20 g fresh truffle, finely chopped
25 ml white truffle oil
100 ml whipping cream,
  semi-whipped

ANY SINEW should be removed from the flesh side of the duck breast. Put the duck into a hot frying pan, skin side down, and cook until golden brown. Turn over and caramelize until golden brown. Turn it again so that it is skin side up, turn down the heat and cook very slowly to render away the fat.

MEANWHILE, heat a baking tray for 30 minutes in a preheated oven at 200°C/400°F/gas 6. Pour away all the fat away from the frying pan, turn the heat back up and add the honey, which will begin to boil immediately. Carefully spoon the honey over the duck and once the honey is caramelized, remove the duck from the pan and place on a wire rack.

OPEN ALL THE WINDOWS and doors, open the oven door and quickly sprinkle the wood chippings on the hot tray. Place the wire rack on top of the chippings and close the oven door. The smoking will take no more than 1½ minutes. Remove the tray from the oven, the wire rack from the tray and place the tray outside to burn out. Put the smoked duck breast in the refrigerator.

PEEL ANY SKIN away from the goat's cheese and crumble it into a food processor, add the chopped truffle and the truffle oil. Blend until smooth and spoon the creamed goat's cheese into a bowl. Gently fold in the semi-whipped cream and set aside.

SLICE THE DUCK BREAST as finely as possible and arrange it on four plates. Spoon the mousse onto the plate and serve with a simple dressed salad and a crouton or toasted bread.

This is a more complicated version of the potato and baked bread soup, but it is visually stunning and will really impress your guests. The potatoes that you use in this recipe must be perfect for deep-frying – some varieties work better than others at different times of the year. 'Chippie's Choice' is a good option – or ask your local greengrocer which varieties are best.

Potato and Chicken Cannelloni with Parmesan Cream

SERVES 4
12 large, three-bone chicken wings
1 litre white chicken stock
   (see page 199)
4 large potatoes
½ quantity chicken mousse
   (see page 214)
2 tablespoons chopped truffle
4 tablespoons shallot confit
   (see page 210)
1 tablespoon finely shredded
   flat leaf parsley
500 ml semi-skimmed milk
½ quantity mashed potato
   (see page 209)
2 tablespoons white truffle oil
olive oil
1 quantity Parmesan cream sauce
   (see page 212)
3 tablespoons whipped cream
100 ml brown chicken stock
   (see page 199)
25 g butter
4 large sprigs of thyme
buckler sorrel leaves, to garnish
salt

PREPARE AND COOK the chicken wings as in Braised Chicken with Sourdough Bread and Potato Soup (see page 102). Set 100 ml chicken stock aside to reheat the wings later.

CUT ONE OF THE POTATOES into 1 cm dice. Blanch these in boiling salted water until soft, refresh in iced water and dry on kitchen paper. Mix the potato dice with the chicken mousse, half the chopped truffle, half the shallot confit and half the parsley. Transfer to a piping bag and keep in the refrigerator.

HEAT THE MILK and whisk in the mashed potato. Add the truffle oil, check the seasoning and add a touch more salt if needed. Pass through a fine sieve and pour into a gas canister, insert a gas cartridge and keep in a pan of warm water to keep warm.

PEEL THE REST OF POTATOES and feed them through a mandolin to give long sheets of potato. Cut the sheets into rectangles, 12 x 8 cm. You will need at least 12, but I would suggest that you prepare extra to allow for casualties along the way.

LINE A TRAY WITH CLINGFILM. Brush one side with olive oil, sprinkle over little salt and lay six rectangles of potato on top. Brush them again with oil. Wrap in clingfilm again and steam for 3–4 minutes until the potato sheets are cooked. Put them in the refrigerator to stop them from cooking. Lay a sheet of clingfilm on your work surface, lay one of the steamed potato rectangles on the clingfilm, with a long side nearest you. Pipe some mousse along the edge nearest to you about 1 cm in from end to end. Using the clingfilm to help, wrap the potato around the mousse to form a cannelloni. Tie up both ends of the clingfilm to seal and place the cannelloni in the refrigerator until you need them.

LAY SIX OF the potato sheets on a flat baking tray lined with greaseproof paper. Season with salt, brush a little oil over each rectangle, lay another sheet of greaseproof over and put another tray on top. Put a weight on top of the second tray, then cook in a preheated oven at 160°C/310°F/gas 2½ for 12–15 minutes. Once cooked and golden brown, transfer to a wire rack to cool.

YOU WILL NEED a stainless steel or copper piping tube for this part of the recipe. Line the tube with greaseproof paper, then wrap the remaining potato sheets around the tube, using butcher's twine to tie the sheets in place. Deep-fry these at 160°C/310°F until they are golden brown. This is when you are likely to have some casualties. Allow the tube to cool down slightly, then remove the string. The paper should help you remove the potato from the tube.

PLACE THE CHICKEN mousse cannelloni into the steamer for 7 minutes, remove the clingfilm and place them on the left-hand side of four plates. Heat the Parmesan cream, mix in the remaining chopped truffle, fold in the whipped cream and spoon the mixture over the cannelloni and around the plates. Put the plates under a preheated hot grill and the Parmesan cream will glaze.

HEAT THE BROWN CHICKEN STOCK and add the remaining shallot confit. Reheat the chicken wings in 100 ml stock, add the butter and reduce the stock by half. Season with a pinch of salt, add the remaining parsley and lay the wings next to the glazed cannelloni. Fill the crisp cannelloni with the potato soup, lay these next to the chicken wings, sit the crisps in between them, spoon over the stock and garnish with buckler sorrel.

This starter is quite robust, and it's perfect for dinner parties because it will benefit from being made a day or so in advance. I made this terrine for my wedding day for 100 people because it's one of those dishes that most people will enjoy. You will need a sturdy terrine mould to make this dish, and you can serve it with country bread and salad leaves.

Chicken, Leek and Truffle Terrine

SERVES 12
500 ml duck fat
10 chicken legs
1 litre white chicken stock
  (see page 199)
150 ml toasted hazelnut oil
100 g chopped truffle
12 new season leeks
2 bunches of chervil, chopped

MELT THE DUCK FAT in a large casserole pan, add the whole chicken legs and cook on the stove over the lowest possible heat for about 3 hours (the meat should flake away from the bone with ease).

MEANWHILE, reduce the chicken stock by two-thirds. Put it in a blender and, while it is still warm, gradually add the hazelnut oil. If you do this with care the oil should emulsify with the stock. Remove from the blender, add the chopped truffle and set aside.

PLACE A VERY LARGE PAN of water on to boil and season with salt. Trim away the outside layers of the leeks and wash thoroughly under cold running water to remove all the soil. Put the leeks in the boiling water and cook for at least 8 minutes; you should be able to pierce the leek easily with a small knife. Once cooked, transfer the leeks to a large bowl of iced water to chill. When they are chilled, squeeze all the water out and place them on kitchen paper to dry. Then season with salt and pepper.

CAREFULLY REMOVE the chicken legs from the fat and place them on a wire rack to drain and cool slightly. Peel the skin away from the legs, pick the meat away from the bones and put it in a large bowl. Bind the chicken stock and hazelnut emulsion with the leg meat, taking care not to break up the meat too much. Season with salt and pepper.

LINE THE TERRINE MOULD with a double layer of clingfilm, allowing some to hang over the edges. Place a 4 cm layer of meat in first and lay leeks on top of the meat. Repeat with another 4 cm layer of meat, another layer of leeks, ending with a layer of meat.

FOLD OVER the excess clingfilm and put a weight (such as a couple of packs of butter) on top of the terrine and put it in the refrigerator for at least 24 hours to set.

SIMPLY SLICE the terrine and serve it with some toasted country bread and dressed salad leaves.

If you love foie gras you'll think that this dish is well worth the effort. Smoking the foie gras adds a wonderful dimension to the dish but you can omit this part of the recipe. You should be able to get some wood chippings from your fishmonger or butcher. It doesn't really matter what type of wood you use as you will be cooking at such a fast and high heat. The foie gras will just taste of the smoke, not the wood.

Roasted Smoked Foie Gras with Onion Mousse

SERVES 4
400 g foie gras
100 g wood chippings
6 baby onions
300 ml white onion and Parmesan
  soup (see page 24)
3 whole eggs, whisked
100 ml brown chicken stock
  (see page 199)
2 tablespoons shallot confit
  (see page 210)
10 ml sherry vinegar
20 leaves of pennywort
  or buckler sorrel
4 slices of sourdough bread,
  toasted
salt

DIP A LONG, thin knife into a pan of hot water and slice the foie gras into four equal slices. Put them on a wire cooling rack and keep in the freezer for a couple of hours – this stops it melting during smoking.

HEAT YOUR OVEN as high as it will go, open all your windows and doors, turn your extractor fan on full and cover up your smoke alarm. Place a baking tray in the bottom of the oven and leave it for 30 minutes so that it is as hot as possible.

SEASON THE FROZEN foie gras with salt and have the wire rack ready to put in the oven. Open the oven door and sprinkle the wood chippings liberally across the baking tray. Close the door for 20 seconds to allow the smoke to build up, and then, standing back as far as you can, open the oven door and place the wire rack and the foie gras over the wood chippings. Close the door immediately and leave for 1½ minutes. Open the oven door and use a double folded oven cloth to remove the tray with the chippings and the foie gras. Take the wood chippings outside and let them burn away on the tray. Place the smoked foie gras in the refrigerator to stop it from cooking.

HALVE THE ONIONS lengthways, skin on. Place cut side down in a hot frying pan until they caramelize. Remove the skin and set aside.

MIX THE SOUP with the three eggs, then pass the mixture through a fine sieve. Readjust the seasoning. Line 4 small moulds with clingfilm and lightly brush with melted butter. Place 3 onion halves in each one and then pour in the egg mixture. Fold over the clingfilm and steam at 85°/185°F for 14 minutes. Alternatively, divide the mixture into four soup bowls, cover the bowls with clingfilm and steam at 90°C/195°F for 9–10 minutes. Keep warm. Heat the brown chicken stock with the shallot confit.

PAN-FRY THE FOIE GRAS in a hot pan and caramelize until golden brown, then transfer to a preheated oven at 180°C/350°F/gas 4 until the foie gras is soft in the centre. Deglaze the pan with the sherry vinegar. Place a slice of foie gras with the white onion custard, spoon over the stock then sprinkle the salad leaves over the foie gras. Serve with warm toasted sourdough bread.

Pineapple and fennel have featured on my menus in various forms over the years, from appetizers to elegant starters – such as this one – and even a dessert with homemade yogurt (see page 174). I quite like to start a tasting menu with this dish and finish with the corresponding dessert so that you start and finish your meal with the same flavours.

Roasted Foie Gras with Fennel and Caramelized Pineapple

SERVES 4
1 large, extra sweet pineapple
    (overripe if possible)
2 large fennel bulbs
100 g sugar
200 ml Pernod
3 star anise, crushed
    in a coffee grinder
15 g butter
10 pink peppercorns
4 slices of grade A foie gras,
    75 g each
sherry vinegar, for seasoning
juice of 1 lemon
salt

PEEL THE PINEAPPLE with a large serrated knife. Cut it in half lengthways and cut one of the halves into four pieces, also lengthways. Remove the core from the pieces that have been quartered and trim them to about 9 cm long.

FEED THE REMAINING pineapple through a vegetable juicer along with both fennel bulbs. Pass this mixture through a fine sieve. Boil 100 ml water with the sugar and add this syrup to the pineapple and fennel juice along with half the Pernod. Churn it in an ice cream machine to make a sorbet.

SEASON THE PINEAPPLE quarters with the powdered star anise, put them in a warm, dry, nonstick pan and cook over a low heat so that the natural sugars in the pineapple caramelize on all sides. Add the butter and pink peppercorns to the pan and turn up the heat. When the butter starts to foam add the remaining Pernod. Carefully use a lighter or blowtorch to flambé the Pernod (remember to turn off your extraction fan first) to burn away the raw alcohol. Cook the pineapple quarters in a preheated oven at 140°C/275°F/gas 1 for 20 minutes, basting and turning occasionally. Keep warm.

SEASON THE FOIE GRAS slices with salt and put them in a hot, dry frying pan. Caramelize on both sides, then finish cooking in a preheated oven at 160°C/310°F/gas 2½ for a few minutes. The foie gras should be soft but still retain its shape. Remove the slices from the oven and season with sherry vinegar.

REMOVE THE PINEAPPLE quarters from the oven, season with a little lemon juice and put them in the centre of four plates. Spoon the caramelized cooking liquor over the roasted pineapple. Arrange the pan-fried foie gras next to the roasted pineapple and add a spoonful of fennel and pineapple sorbet.

Why not? People have been serving game with red fruits for years, and there is a classic venison dish that contains bitter chocolate, so it seems fitting to include this recipe in this book. The dish is quite rich and makes a good main course.

Black Forest Pigeon

SERVES 4
300 g fresh black cherries
2 squab pigeons, 550 g each
300 ml duck fat
vegetable oil
100 ml brown chicken stock
  (see page 199)
100 g bitter chocolate, chopped
salt and pepper

PIT ALL THE CHERRIES. Finely chop two-thirds of them and put them in a small saucepan with a little water. Cover and cook until they are very soft. Pass the purée through a fine sieve and keep warm in a small, clean pan.

REMOVE THE LEGS from the pigeons and cook them in duck fat in a preheated oven at 80°C/180°F/gas ¼ for at least 2 hours. Remove the head, neck and backbone from the pigeon. Season the remaining crown with salt and pepper and place them in a hot ovenproof frying pan. Add a little vegetable oil and caramelize on both sides. This should take around 3 minutes for each side. Finish cooking by roasting in a preheated oven at 180°C/350°F/gas 4 for a further 5 minutes. Remove the birds from the oven and allow them to rest, breast down, for at least 5 minutes.

REHEAT THE CHICKEN STOCK and add the remaining pitted cherries. Reheat the cherry purée and mix in the bitter chocolate until it has melted.

REMOVE THE PIGEON LEGS from the duck fat and season with salt. Quickly reheat the pigeon breasts in the oven.

REMOVE THE BREASTS from the carcass and arrange on four plates with the legs. Spoon the cherry and chocolate purée onto the plates and dress with the cherry and chocolate jus.

I've been cooking one variation or another of this dish ever since I was 22 years old. It has now developed into quite a complicated main course and has been influenced by the chefs I have worked with over the years. But the staple ingredients have remained the same: cabbage, pigeon and sweet garlic butter. The balance of acidity and sweetness is perfect. It is best to start the pickled cabbage a couple of days in advance.

Squab Pigeon with Pickled Cabbage and Sweet Garlic Butter Sauce

SERVES 4

2 squab pigeons (make sure the legs are fully intact and not broken), 550 g each
50 g foie gras
12 slices of Ventreche bacon
20 ml balsamic vinegar
4 tablespoons shallot confit (see page 210)
100 g duck fat
3 garlic cloves, sliced
2 large Desiree potatoes
1 quantity pigeon mousse (see page 215)
1 quantity sweet garlic butter sauce (see page 212), reserving a little of the garlic confit for garnish
1 quantity pigeon sauce (see page 215)
4 juniper berries
salt and pepper

PICKLED CABBAGE

½ white cabbage
2 large onions
200 g duck fat
4 juniper berries
4 garlic cloves, sliced
good handful of parsley stalk and thyme (tied together with string)
150 ml white wine vinegar
150 ml white wine
sea salt (optional)

MAKE THE PICKLED CABBAGE. Slice the white cabbage and the onion as finely as possible, ideally using a mandolin. Bring a large pan of water with a good handful of salt to the boil. Heat another large pan and add the duck fat. Cook the onions in the fat without letting them colour, add the juniper berries, garlic, parsley stalks and thyme. Blanch the cabbage in the boiling salted water and transfer immediately to the cooked onions. Cover the pan and cook for 5 minutes. Remove the lid, add the white wine vinegar and reduce by half. Add the white wine and cook for 1 hour, season with sea salt if needed.

PREPARE THE PIGEONS. Cut away the head and neck. Turn the bird upside down and run your knife down the backbone. Turn it over again and cut the skin between the leg and the breast, dislocate the tibia bone from the carcass and remove all the skin and the leg away from the carcass. The idea is to keep as much skin as possible attached to the legs. Cut away all but the middle pigeon toe and remove any leftover feathers. Lay out the legs, skin side down, and remove the tibia with a small knife and set aside.

REMOVE THE WING from the breast, leaving the first bone attached to the breast. Trim away the tip of the wing and keep this for the stock. You should now be left with the middle bone of the wing. Remove the back from the carcass so that you are just left with the crown. Set aside. Open up the carcass and remove the livers. Finely dice the livers and set aside.

DICE THE FOIE GRAS and eight slices of bacon. In a hot frying pan add the bacon dice and cook for 1–2 minutes, add the foie gras and pigeon livers and stir well. Season with salt and the balsamic vinegar, stir in the shallot confit and set aside to cool.

WHEN IT IS COOL spoon this mixture into the centre of the boned-out legs and wrap the excess skin around the mixture to form the shape of your finger. Wrap these fingers in clingfilm and tie the end into a knot to secure the filling.

PLACE THE WRAPPED and stuffed pigeon legs and the pigeon wings in the duck fat and cook for at least 3 hours on as low a heat as possible. After 1 hour add the garlic cloves to the duck fat before you remove the wings.

WHEN THE WINGS are cooked you will be able to push the two bones out. (This may seem like a lot of work but it is an example of how you can use up the whole bird, but, of course, you could skip it altogether if you prefer.) Put the stuffed legs on a wire rack with another tray underneath to catch any excess duck fat, remove the clingfilm with a pair of scissors and rewrap the pigeon legs in clingfilm to keep their shape. Transfer to the refrigerator and allow the meat to set into shape. Once set remove the clingfilm.

SEASON THE CROWNS heavily with salt and pepper and put them in a small, hot frying pan and seal them on both sides. This will take about 3 minutes, then finish the cooking in a preheated oven at 180°C/350°F/gas 4, breast side down, for 10 minutes. Leave the crowns to rest for at least 10 minutes.

FEED THE PEELED potato through a mandolin with a fine shredder attachment. Wrap the potato around the pigeon legs and deep-fry until golden brown. Cut away the bottom so the leg can stand up.

REHEAT THE CROWNS for a couple of minutes. With the cooked birds sitting on your board breasts upwards, run your knife down either side of the breastbone, keeping as close to the bone as possible. Simply peel away the breast away from the carcass using the knife to help you ease the meat away. When you reach the wing bone make sure that this bone comes away with the breast.

TO SERVE, place some mousse on four plates and spoon the sweet garlic butter sauce over each portion. Put pickled cabbage on the plates and place the pigeon breast on top. Reheat the pigeon sauce with the garlic confit and the pigeon wing inside. Arrange them on the plates with the deep-fried legs, spoon the sauce over the breast and dress with the bacon crisp.

This delicious but simple salad can be used for either a starter or a main course. Take care when you are removing the skin from the bark pumpkin because these pumpkins have very tough skins and your knife could very easily slip. I suggest that you use a serrated pastry knife if you have one.

Warm Wood Pigeon Salad
with Roasted Pumpkin and Sage

SERVES 4
300 ml duck fat
4 oven-ready wood pigeons
¼ bark pumpkin
50 ml olive oil
100 g butter
½ bunch of sage
10 g toasted pumpkin seeds
50 ml honey
juice of 1 lemon
vegetable oil
buckler sorrel and wood
   sorrel leaves, to serve
rock salt
cracked black pepper

GENTLY HEAT THE DUCK fat on the stove but do not allow it to boil. Remove the legs from the pigeons and put them in the duck fat. Season with some rock salt and cook the legs on top of the stove for a couple of hours. When the meat flakes easily away from the leg, take the legs from the fat and allow them to cool slightly before you pick the meat away from the bone. Put the meat in a bowl, cover with clingfilm and set aside.

CAREFULLY PEEL THE SKIN away from the bark pumpkin and cut it into even pieces. Heat a large, nonstick, ovenproof frying pan and add half the olive oil. Put the pumpkin pieces in the pan, season with salt and cracked black pepper, then cook to caramelize the pumpkin on all sides. Add the butter and sage leaves and then cook in a preheated oven at 170°C/325°F/gas 3 for about 20 minutes or until the pumpkin is soft. Turn the pieces while they are in the oven, basting the pieces with the sage butter. Remove the pumpkin from the oven and leave the pumpkin in the pan until you need it.

TOAST THE PUMPKIN seeds lightly in a pan on the stove, add the honey and caramelize lightly. Remove from the heat, add the lemon juice, the remaining olive oil and the flaked leg meat.

HEAT ANOTHER OVENPROOF frying pan. Season the pigeons with salt and pepper. Add a little vegetable oil to the pan and add the birds. Cook to caramelize for a minute or so on each breast, and then roast the birds in a preheated oven at 180°C/350°F/gas 4 for 3 minutes. Remove the birds from the oven and leave to rest for 5 minutes, breast downwards.

USE A SMALL, sharp knife to peel the skin away from the flesh. Put the bird and the pumpkin back into the oven to reheat. When they are warm, arrange the pumpkin pieces on four plates. Return the pan to the stove and the sage butter will foam again, remove the breasts from the birds and toss breasts in the sage butter. Arrange on the plates (two breasts on each plate), spoon a little of the sage butter over the breast and the pumpkin pieces. Scatter the leg meat and pumpkin seeds over the plates and then add the sorrel leaves.

Duck and orange with a twist! A lot of people say they don't like chicory because of its bitterness but here it's cooked and sweetened until most of the bitterness is gone. The carrot and orange purée seemed like a natural combination.

Breast of Mallard with Sweetened Chicory and Carrot Purée

SERVES 4
10 g butter
25 g caster sugar
2 large white chicory endive
500 g young carrots
2 star anise
2 large sprigs of tarragon
juice of 6 orange
juice of 1 lemon (optional)
2 mallards
salt and pepper

COAT A COLD, flat-bottomed pan with butter and sprinkle some sugar onto the butter, making sure that all the butter is coated. Cut the chicory in half lengthways and lay the pieces cut side down in the pan. Cover with a sheet of greaseproof paper and place over a very low heat – the longer you cook the chicory, the less bitter it becomes. Cook the chicory for 3–4 hours and try not to disturb them by moving them around while they cook. If you do see them caramelizing too much turn the heat down even more, add a little orange juice and replace the paper. Once they are cooked they should have no crunch left in them and should be golden brown. Leave them in the pan until you need them.

PEEL THE CARROTS and chop them as finely as possible. Put them in a warm pan with the remaining butter, the star anise and tarragon and a little salt. Cover and cook over quite a fierce heat – the quicker you cook the purée the fresher it will taste. Stir frequently so that it does not burn. After about 5 minutes and when the carrots are becoming soft, remove the lid, add the orange juice and reduce over a fierce heat. Remove the star anise and tarragon and blend the carrot mixture in a blender until smooth. Pass it through a fine sieve and check the seasoning. The orange should give it the sweetness and acidity it needs, but if not add a little sugar and some lemon juice. Keep warm.

SEASON THE DUCKS generously with salt and pepper and put them in a hot, ovenproof frying pan with a little oil. Caramelize both breasts evenly, which should take 3–4 minutes per breast, then place the ducks in a preheated oven at 180°C/350°F/gas 4 for about 6 minutes (this will take the duck to medium rare). Allow the duck to rest, breast side down, for at least 10 minutes.

PLACE THE DUCK back in the hot oven to reheat for a couple of minutes, then remove the breasts from the carcass.

SPOON THE CARROT PURÉE onto the plates, reheat the chicory briefly in the oven and lay on the plates, caramelized side up. Slice the duck breast and arrange it on the plates. Spoon some of the syrup from the chicory over the sliced duck breast.

Of all the game birds, teal is my favourite. Its strong, distinctive flavour makes it superior, in my opinion, to the likes of grouse and woodcock. This recipe is a simple way to prepare and enjoy this magnificent game bird.

Teal with Orange and Warm Prune Salad

SERVES 4
12 pitted prunes
juice of 4 oranges
4 oven-ready teal
2 oranges, segmented
salad leaves, such as chicco
   rosso, dandelion or chicory
1 quantity orange vinaigrette
   (see page 211)
salt and pepper

WARM THE PRUNES in the orange juice and allow them to cool in the juice.

SINGE ALL THE HAIRS from the teal breast with a gas blowtorch. Season generously with salt and pepper. Place the breasts in a hot ovenproof frying pan, with a little vegetable oil, and seal both breasts for a minute or so (there is no need to render away the fat because these ducks are so small that the don't carry any fat). Transfer the teal to finish cooking in a preheated oven at 180°C/350°F/gas 4 for about 4 minutes. Remove the teal from the oven and leave them to rest for 5 minutes with the breast side downwards.

ARRANGE THE ORANGE segments on the four plates. Add the warm prunes. Dress the salad leaves with the orange vinaigrette. Carve the breasts away from the carcasses and season again with a pinch of salt. Place the salad leaves on the plates and lay the breasts on top.

Hare is my favourite game, and serving it with a hotpot and autumn vegetables really brings home the rustic nature of the meat. Hare fillet has an amazing taste and texture: the flavour is similar to venison but it is smoother in texture. It's a shame that hare is usually associated only with stews and other slow-cooked dishes. For the tenderest meat, hare is best cooked when young and hung for a few days. The legs and saddle make the choicest cuts.

Saddle of Hare with Autumn Vegetables and Hare Hotpot

SERVES 4
4 large onions
175 g unsalted butter
10 large sprigs of thyme
2 large carrots
1 head of garlic
2 large hares
flour
100 ml vegetable oil
350 ml red wine
350 ml port
300 ml veal stock (see page 202)
4 very thin slices of smoked bacon
20 sage leaves
4 large potatoes, peeled and sliced
12 leaves of chicory endive
½ quantity artichoke cooking liquor
  (see page 198)
50 g chicken livers, puréed
4 large carrots from the bunch
4 sticks of salsify
2 large parsnips
salt and pepper

MAKE THE HOTPOT. Peel and slice two onions as finely as possible. In a warm covered pan slowly sweat the onions in 100 g butter with four thyme sprigs and a sprinkle of salt until the onions are very soft. Remove the lid and continue cooking for 30–40 minutes. When the onions are golden brown, check the seasoning. You should be able to taste the salt and the natural sweetness of the onions should also come forward. Pour the onions onto a tray to cool down.

PEEL AND COARSELY CHOP the carrots, garlic and the remaining onions. Cook in a large casserole pan in a little oil and 25 g butter, add six sprigs of thyme and caramelize for a further 2 minutes or so. Drain away the excess butter, leaving the vegetables in the pan.

REMOVE THE BACK LEGS from the hare, season with salt and pepper and coat them lightly in flour. Put them in a hot frying pan with vegetable oil and caramelize well. Remove from the oil and place on the caramelized vegetables. Cover with the red wine and port, cook to reduce by two-thirds and add the veal stock. Cover with a sheet of greaseproof paper and a tight-fitting lid and cook in a preheated oven at 140°C/275°F/gas 1 for 3 hours or until soft.

REMOVE THE LID and paper, take the hare legs from the braising liquor, place them on a tray and cover with clingfilm to stop the meat from drying out. When the legs are cool enough to handle, flake the meat away from the bones, checking carefully for any shattered bones or pellet shots. Pass the cooking liquor through a fine sieve into a saucepan, bring it to the boil and pass it through muslin. Reduce the stock by half, tasting continuously as the salt from the legs may become too strong the more it reduces.

WHEN THE LIQUOR is reduced to your liking, pass it through muslin again and pour some of the liquor onto the flaked leg meat. Place this meat in the bottom of four ovenproof dishes, about 1½ cm deep. Lay a thin slice of smoked bacon on top, then a thin layer of the caramelized onions. Add two sage leaves to each pot and then layer the sliced potatoes on top of the onions. Sprinkle the potatoes with a little salt and pepper, then pour a couple spoonfuls of the strained braising

liquor over the potatoes. Cook in a preheated oven at 160°C/310°F/ gas 2½ for 35–40 minutes, covering each pot for the first 10 minutes, then removing it for the remainder of the cooking time.

PREPARE THE HARE LOIN. Trim the hare loin away from the saddle and then trim away the silver sinew.

BLANCH THE CHICORY LEAVES in the artichoke cooking liquor for 4 minutes and allow the liquor to cool with the leaves in it. When it is cool, remove the leaves and put them on kitchen paper to dry. Lay a sheet of clingfilm on to your work surface and lay four chicory leaves next to each other, placing them lengthways.

SPREAD THE PURÉED chicken livers over the chicory, lay the hare loin down on the chicory, place two sage leaves on each loin and then use the clingfilm to help you wrap the chicory around the loin. Tie both ends of the clingfilm, as if tying a sausage. Leave to rest in the refrigerator for 4–5 hours.

UNWRAP THE CLINGFILM from the loin, taking care that the chicory remains attached to the meat. Heat a nonstick frying pan, add a little vegetable oil, season the loin with salt and gently place into the pan. Cook for 3–4 minutes to caramelize the chicory on all sides until golden brown, then place in a preheated oven at 180°C/350°F/gas 4 for no more than 2 minutes. Transfer to a wire rack and allow to rest.

PREPARE THE BRAISED VEGETABLES. Peel the carrots, salsify and parsnips and cut them into even shapes. Put them into a hot frying pan with 50 g butter, four sage leaves and a good pinch of salt. Cook over a very low heat, turning the vegetables continuously until they are evenly cooked. Drain away any excess butter, add 100 ml of the hare braising liquor and leave to cook for a further 2–3 minutes.

TO SERVE, reheat the hotpots in the oven for a few minutes. Reheat the loin for no more than 30 seconds, place it on a chopping board and carve each one into three slices. Place these on four plates with the braised vegetables. Spoon the leftover jus over the hare loin and serve the hotpots on the side.

Veal rump is a fantastic piece of meat. It's also cheaper than the more common and expensive veal loin. If the rump is cooked to no more than medium rare, I believe that it's better than the loin. However, if you want your meat cooked more than medium rare then I suggest you opt for the loin.

Rump of Veal with Spaghetti and Spring Vegetables

SERVES 4
600 g veal rump
20 ml vegetable oil
20 ml olive oil
½ quantity fresh pasta
(see page 208)
2 large Italian bunch carrots
100 g podded fresh peas
100 g podded fresh broad beans
150 ml veal stock (see page 202)
75 g butter
3 tablespoons shallot confit
(see page 210)
200 ml white chicken stock
(see page 199)
2 tablespoons of chopped
flat leaf parsley
10 mint leaves, chopped
juice of 1 lemon
salt and pepper

TRIM AWAY ANY EXCESS sinew and fat from the veal and cut it into four equal pieces. Heat a large, ovenproof frying pan and add a little vegetable oil. Season the veal with salt and pepper, seal the meat in the pan until evenly caramelized and then cook it in a preheated oven at 180°C/350°F/gas 4 for 20 minutes or until the centre of the meat reaches 40–43°C/100°F. Allow the meat to rest on a wire rack for at least 10 minutes before reheating to serve.

PLACE A LARGE PAN of water on to boil, add a good handful of salt and a dash of olive oil. Have ready a colander in the sink, a bowl of iced water and a carving fork. Roll the pasta through a pasta machine, twice on each setting to stop the pasta from stretching and shrinking before cooking. Heavily flour the pasta while you are working it through the machine. Allow the dough to sit for a couple of minutes until it dries out slightly; this will help stop the pasta getting caught up in the fine spaghetti attachment on the pasta machine. Pass all the pasta through the spaghetti attachment. Plunge it into the boiling water and stir with a carving fork to help stop it sticking together. Cook the pasta for no more than 40 seconds, then drain through the colander and plunge immediately into iced water, again stirring the pasta to stop it sticking together. Drain and place on a tray, mix with a little olive oil, cover with clingfilm and place in the refrigerator until needed.

PEEL AND SLICE the carrots lengthways on a mandolin. Blanch all the vegetables in boiling salted water. Chill immediately in iced water, drain and set aside.

REHEAT THE VEAL rump in the oven for a couple of minutes. Reduce the veal stock by half, add half the butter and all the shallot confit. Coat the rump in the reduced stock.

REDUCE THE CHICKEN stock by half, add the remaining butter and boil it until it emulsifies. Add the blanched vegetables, pasta and chopped fresh herbs, season with a little lemon juice and salt if needed.

DIVIDE THE PASTA and vegetables among four bowls and place the veal rump on top of the pasta.

DOWN ON THE FARM

Meat production in the British Isles has for many years been driven by economic considerations – the requirement to produce animals, which grow faster but eat less food, and by an overriding obsession with leanness in meat. The result has been meat which may look good on the sales counter but which is often tough and tasteless. Modern beef is usually bright red, has not been hung for any length of time and has been sourced from any breed of cattle which fits the requirement for cheap, lean meat.

Those of us who love to eat and cook meat have shunned intensive farming methods by using consumer power. This has encouraged better meat on the market: naturally fed, slower grown animals that are not stocked in high densities and that are far more resistant to disease. These animals also taste better as they are not stressed. There is scientific proof that stressed animals produce meat of poor eating quality.

My in-laws, Gillian and Tony, have for years bought own-brand food products and enjoyed a last minute supermarket bargain. When they have eaten with us they have been so impressed with the difference in flavour and texture of the rare breed Middle White pork or the hand-reared chicken that now they have dramatically converted into organic, free range eating fans.

Not only is the meat a damn sight more enjoyable to eat, it can also give you the feel-good factor that you are doing something towards the change that is necessary. For another healthy attitude to meat, take inspiration from the time when meat was considered a luxury and cooks had to be clever in the ways that they used it.

Huntsham Farm Pedigree Meats is owned and run by Richard Vaughan and his wife, Rosamund. It specialises in producing the finest meat from rare pedigree animals – Longhorn beef, Middle White pork and Ryeland lamb – rather than just beef, pork and lamb. I visited Huntsham Farm to see for myself how Richard manages his farm, situated in the beautiful Wye valley. The farm has been in the Vaughan family for nearly four hundred years.

Richard has gone from being a mass producer of unethically farmed meat – where he would make plenty of money with very little effort – to a producer of some of the finest beef and pork that is available in Great Britain.

Huntsham meat has been produced with superior taste and texture as the primary consideration. It therefore has a higher fat content than most intensively farmed meat, which greatly enhances its taste and succulence. Some people like to eat the fat, others don't, but it is important that the meat is cooked with its fat. Those who don't like fat should look on it like the sediment in a good bottle of wine – you don't drink it but it needs to be there.

His approach to animal feed is similarly straightforward; free from the growth promoters often fed to intensively farmed pigs, it's a mix of cereals, soya bean meals, peas and beans – all top sources of pig-friendly protein. That neither the feed, nor Richard's farming methods, are organic clearly hasn't been a problem for the top chefs who buy from him – I believe Richard's Middle White has a flavour that surpasses even the finest of organically reared pigs.

And, as for the bog standard pork you'll find on most supermarket shelves, there's no comparison. That kind of pork comes from pigs bred for bacon, whose more muscular, leaner meat is fine for rashers but just can't supply the succulent, unctuous taste and texture you need for a decent cut of pork. No fat, no flavour, it's that simple.

Richard's husbandry techniques also have a huge role to play. His philosophy is simple: give them a happy life. Unlike intensively farmed pigs, which are frequently kept in the smallest space legally allowed, Huntsham pigs have the run of the farm. When the weather's good, they're out grazing the fields with the Longhorn beef and Ryeland lamb (both rare breeds). When it's bad they shelter in barns supplied with plenty of straw for bedding and recreation.

Richard no longer counts supermarkets among his customers – he just can't produce enough. Not that he's worried. Richard says, 'If the supermarkets say, "we'll pay you x pence a kilo", then it's down to me to bring my costs down below x pence a kilo to make any kind of a profit. Instead, we ask ourselves what we need to spend to make a quality product, then price accordingly. Our only consideration is producing meat that people think is delicious'.

Sadly, veal isn't popular in Britain. Even many hardened carnivores won't eat it, and it accounts for a mere 0.1 per cent of the meat bought in Britain. Fewer than one in a hundred households buys and eats it. White veal, which is not produced in Britain, has been rightly branded as cruel. The calf is confined to a crate to restrict its movement and atrophy the muscles. This, combined with a liquid diet low in iron and roughage, makes the meat tender and pale. Crating has been illegal in Britain since 1990, but although crates were banned throughout Europe in 2007, slatted floors, which make it difficult for the calves to stand up, are still allowed, and the space allowed to each animal remains relatively small. The dietary fibre in their diet is still less than the British minimum requirement.

British veal, however, is produced to the highest welfare standards, and has pink, not white flesh and it is tender and delicately flavoured. Called rosé veal,

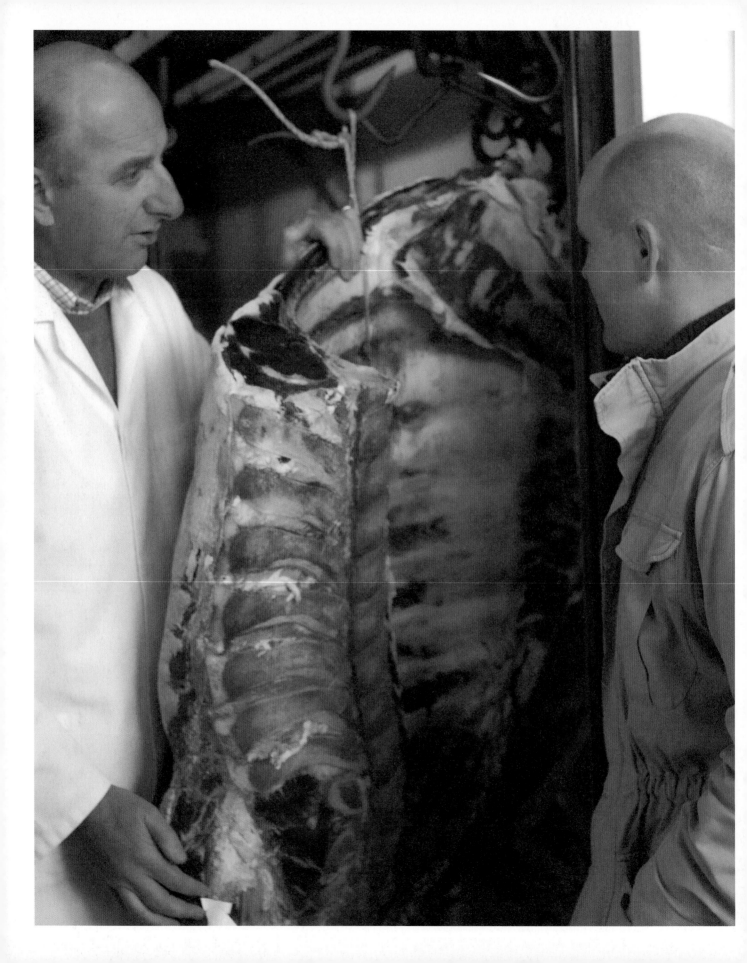

it is the meat for the conscientious meat eater. The mothers suckle their calves, and they eat natural food and live outdoors in the summer months. The calves live for about six months, enjoying a longer life than many pigs. The RSPCA gives high-welfare veal its approval with its Freedom Food label and would like more meat-eaters to buy it. But production is driven by demand, and until demand grows unwanted dairy calves will continue to be shot or exported.

The true world of meat is hundreds of different cuts and ten times as many recipes. The ingenuity behind some recipes that use lesser-known cuts is astounding, and the ability to make them is a virtue to value. There's an excellent motive for bringing back the knack of knowing what to do with cuts beyond the steak. They are often better value than the popular leaner varieties, and you are at the beginning of discovering dozens of new recipes, which in turn allows the farmer to sell to the consumer, the whole of the animal instead of just the prime parts.

Meat scares dominated the end of last century, but the positive outcome has been an increase in consumer interest in high-quality meat, inspiring farmers to promote their high standards of animal welfare and natural rearing techniques. Loyalty from you the consumer for the best meat that the country can produce will help promote more farmers like Richard Vaughan and encourage a greater variety of cuts, that cost less and taste incredible.

I now believe that this generation has a responsibility to feed their children the best available produce there is. If our children watch us make that change then they will follow suit. Our grandparents and parents opened packets of processed foods, because that is all that was available throughout and after the war, but now we have no excuses, all we need is readily available, all we have to do is change our mind set.

When I started cooking, the accepted way of cooking a veal shin was to cut it into pieces and braise it, osso bucco style. Things have moved on, and chefs are now using this fantastic piece of meat in all shapes and forms: stuffed into ravioli, served with shellfish or simply placed in the middle of a family table with a pile of thyme mashed potato and seasonal vegetables. The foreleg is best to use because the shin is smaller and easier to work with.

Braised Veal Shin

SERVES AT LEAST 6
1 whole veal shin (about 4 kg),
   untrimmed
150 ml vegetable oil
4 large carrots
2 large onions
1 whole head of garlic
1 bunch of thyme
rock salt
cracked pepper

YOU WILL NEED the largest roasting tray that your oven will take. Ask your butcher to trim the bone down from the foot end so that the whole shin will fit in your oven. Put the shin in the roasting tray, coat it with vegetable oil and season with rock salt and cracked pepper. Cook it in a preheated oven at 140°C/275°F/gas 1 for about 1 hour. Turn the shin over after 30 minutes so that it caramelizes evenly all over. Remove the shin from the tray and set aside. Increase the oven temperature to 180°C/350°F/gas 4.

PEEL AND CUT THE CARROTS, onions and garlic in half. Put them directly into the roasting tray that the shin has just come out of, toss them in the hot oil and cook in the oven at 180°C/350°F/gas 4 for about 20 minutes.

PUT THE VEAL SHIN in a casserole pan that is large enough for you to cover it completely with water. Add the roasted vegetables and the thyme. Place over a high heat and allow to come to the boil. Skim any excess grease from the top, turn down to a simmer and allow to cook for at least 2 hours.

CAREFULLY REMOVE the shin from the pan, and continue to cook the stock for a further hour. Remove the vegetables, pass the stock through a fine sieve and then through a muslin cloth. Return the stock to the pan and reduce by two-thirds. Put the shin back in the pan with the reduced stock, cover and reheat. Bring the casserole to the table, carve and serve.

Oxtail is, I believe, incredibly flavoursome. You will need to marinade the oxtail for 24 hours before cooking this dish. Be cheeky and ask your butcher for the largest pieces he has. You will be grateful of your boldness later when you're trying to flake the meat away from the tail. This could be served as a starter with an onion soup or as a garnish with a medium rare steak and some mashed potato.

Braised Oxtail Wrapped in Caul Fat with Braised Winter Vegetables

SERVES 4

3 kg oxtail pieces, trimmed
½ quantity chicken mousse
  (see page 214)
100 g caul fat, soaked in cold
  water for 2 hours

MARINADE

2 carrots, peeled and roughly
  chopped
1 onion, peeled and roughly
  chopped
3 garlic cloves, split and roughly
  chopped
1 bottle of red wine
4 bay leaves
10 peppercorns
8 sprigs of thyme

FOR BRAISING

1 tablespoon vegetable oil
50 g butter
2 large carrots, peeled and chopped
1 head of garlic, cut widthways
25 g smoked bacon, diced
2 onions, peeled and chopped
8 sprigs of thyme
3 bay leaves
50 g flour
1 bottle of red wine
500 ml veal stock (see page 202)
salt and pepper

BRAISED VEGETABLES

2 large carrots, peeled
1 large parsnip, peeled
1 medium sized turnip, peeled
50 g butter
4 sprigs of thyme

MAKE THE MARINADE. Mix all the ingredients together in a large bowl and add the oxtail. Place in the refrigerator for 24 hours.

REMOVE THE OXTAIL from the marinade and leave to dry. Meanwhile, place a large casserole pan on the heat. Add a little vegetable oil to the hot pan, then add the butter, carrots, garlic and smoked bacon and caramelize slightly. Add the onion, thyme and bay leaves, caramelize these slightly and then pour into a colander to drain away the fat. Add some fresh oil to the same hot pan, season the oxtail with salt and pepper, coat the pieces in the flour and brown in the pan. Reduce the heat slightly as the flavour of the oxtail will benefit from a slow cooking. When the oxtail is fully caramelized, drain it in a colander, then return the vegetables and oxtail to the pan, cover with the red wine and reduce by half over a high heat. Add the veal stock, bring to the boil, cover and cook in a preheated oven at 120°C/230°F/gas ½ for at least 4 hours, or until the meat comes away from the tail easily.

POUR THE BRAISING LIQUID through a colander, then through a fine sieve and then through muslin a couple of times. Put it in a saucepan and reboil. Skim away any excess fat and residue that comes to the top. Pick the meat from the bone, taking care that you remove any cartilage that has come away from the bone. Set all the picked meat aside.

PREPARE THE BRAISED VEGETABLES. Cut the carrot, turnip and parsnip into 1 cm dice. Heat a large frying pan, add a little vegetable oil and the butter and thyme sprigs. Add the diced vegetables and slowly caramelize in the foaming butter. Season with salt and pepper. Once cooked, drain away the butter, add some of the oxtail braising liquor and cook for a further 5 minutes.

COOL THE VEGETABLES SLIGHTLY and mix them with the picked oxtail meat. Add 100 ml of the reduced braising liquor to the mixture and allow them all to cool together. When they are cold, fold in the chicken mousse, roll the mixture into evenly sized balls and totally cover each ball with the caul fat. Place them on a buttered baking tray, pour some of the braising liquor over and bake in a preheated oven at 160°C/310°F/gas 2½ for 10–12 minutes. Serve with the braised vegetables and a little juice spooned over.

This is one of my favourite dishes. Veal isn't popular in Britain but few are aware that British veal is produced to the highest standards in Europe, with the animal's welfare a high priority. The result is the delicious rosé veal which has pink, not white, flesh.

Veal Cutlets with Broad Beans and Girolle Mushrooms

SERVES 4
2 large rosé veal cutlets
4 kg large, waxy potatoes, such as Cara, Charlottes or Nicola
4 kg broad beans in their shells
1 kg Scottish girolles
vegetable oil
50 g butter
4 large sprigs of thyme
100 ml white port
300 ml veal stock (see page 202)
100 ml double cream
small bunch chervil, chopped
salt and pepper

THE VEAL CUTLETS should be well trimmed to remove any sinew and tied so that they maintain their shape during cooking. Season the meat.

USE A SMALL KNIFE to shape the potatoes into cocottes (resembling small eggs) and keep them in cold water.

POD AND BLANCH the broad beans in plenty of boiling salted water for about 1½ minutes. Plunge them immediately into iced water to stop them from cooking further. Remove the shells and set aside.

CLEAN THE MUSHROOM by removing any soil and scraping down the base with a small knife to expose the clean stem.

HEAT A LARGE CASSEROLE PAN, add a little oil and half the butter. Add the veal and cook to caramelize on all sides until golden brown. Remove the meat and the potatoes to the same pan. Caramelize again until golden brown, then add the mushrooms and thyme. Cook for a further minute. Remove the potatoes and the mushrooms from the pan and drain away the butter. Return the veal to the pan, and then add the potatoes, thyme and mushrooms. Add the port and reduce by half.

ADD THE VEAL STOCK, bring to the boil then cover the casserole and cook in a preheated oven at 170°C/325°F/gas 3 for 5 minutes. Remove from the oven and allow the meat to rest inside the casserole for 10 minutes. Remove the meat and cut it into four cutlets.

MEANWHILE, add the cream to the pan and reduce by half. Add the blanched broad beans and a handful of chopped chervil and the remaining butter. Bring back to the boil.

SERVE THE MEAT sliced and simply pile the garnish next to it, pouring the sauce over the meat.

I've included one variation or another of this dish on my menus for as long as I can remember. I love the way the delicate and intense ingredients come together in a controlled manner. Although the recipe can be put together without too much difficulty, it is a really luxurious dish.

Veal Fillet with Lobster, Apple Fondants and Jabugo Ham

SERVES 4
2 native lobsters, 500 g each
4 slices of Jabugo ham
4 thin slices of Jabugo ham fat
6 large red apples
1 kg large, waxy potatoes, such
  as Cara, Charlottes or Nicola
250 g butter
4 large sprigs of thyme
1/2 rosé veal fillet, about 400 g
vegetable oil
juice of 1 lemon
150 g veal sweetbreads
  (from the heart, optional)
flour
200 ml veal stock (see page 202)
1 large sprig of rosemary, chopped
buckler sorrel leaves, to serve
salt and pepper

PREPARE AND BLANCH the lobsters as in Lobster with Morels and Tarragon Gnocchi (see page 57). Wrap each tail in a slice of ham, cut the tails in half widthways and then tie in place with string. Wrap each claw in a slice of the Jabugo ham fat.

LEAVING THE SKIN on the apples, use a 1.5 cm pastry cutter to cut out 12 cylinders, avoiding the core. Do the same with the potato. Put the potato cylinders in a small pan with 50 g butter and the thyme and cook over a medium heat until the butter begins to foam. Season with a little salt and turn down the heat to as low as possible and cook for as long as it takes for the potatoes to turn evenly golden brown in colour and to become soft and tender. When the potatoes are cooked, remove them from the pan, add 150 g butter and add the apples to the pan. Repeat the same process, but the apples will take about a quarter of the time it took to cook the potatoes. When the apples are cooked return the potatoes to the butter in the pan to keep them moist.

MAKE SURE YOU REMOVE all sinew and fat from the veal. Season the fillet and put it in a hot frying pan with a little vegetable oil and seal it until it is golden brown all over. The fillet will be half-cooked by now. Finish cooking in a preheated oven at 180°C/350°F/gas 4 for about 3 minutes. Remove the fillet from the oven, place it on a wire rack and leave it to rest for at least 10 minutes before reheating to serve.

PEEL THE SKIN AWAY from the remaining apples, chop the flesh fairly small and cook in a frying pan with a knob of butter for 10–15 minutes over a medium to low heat. Transfer the cooked and caramelized apple to a blender and blend until smooth, add a little lemon juice and salt and pass through a fine sieve. Put the mixture into a clean saucepan, cover with clingfilm and keep warm.

CUT AWAY THE SINEW from the veal sweetbreads and cut them into nuggets a little bit bigger than the potatoes. Coat them lightly in seasoned flour and cook them in a hot pan with vegetable oil to caramelize on all sides until golden brown. Add a knob of butter, a little lemon juice and a sprinkle of salt and remove them to kitchen paper.

PUT THE LOBSTER TAIL in the same hot pan as the sweetbreads and caramelize on all sides, then cook in the oven at 180°C/350°F/gas 4 for 2 minutes. Season with salt and a little lemon juice, remove the string and cut each tail into four slices. Keep the oil from the pan.

REHEAT THE VEAL STOCK and, while it is boiling, whisk in the remaining 50 g butter. Add the rosemary and the lobster oil from the pan. Do not let it boil again. Reheat the veal fillet, the sweetbreads, the potato and apple cylinders and the lobster tail and claw. Spoon the apple purée onto the plate, cut the veal to give five slices for each serving. Arrange the other elements on the plates around the purée. Spoon the sauce over the meat and garnish with buckler sorrel.

The time I spent in Ireland was very important to me. I met some of my closest friends, had lots of fun (of course) and was inspired by the wonderful raw ingredients they have over there.

Beef in Guinness with Watercress and Oysters

SERVES 4

1 kg beef flank (or skirt)
50 g smoked bacon
6 bay leaves
½ bunch of thyme
4 x 300 ml cans of Guinness
1 tablespoon vegetable oil
2 carrots, peeled and chopped
2 onions, peeled and chopped
1 head of garlic, cut in half
  widthways
plain flour
2 litres veal stock (see page 202)
4 portions of beef fillet, 150 g each
100 g watercress purée
  (see page 203)
6 large native oysters

TRIM THE SINEW from the beef flank and put the meat in a large container with the smoked bacon, bay leaves, thyme and Guinness. Cover and leave in the refrigerator for 24 hours.

REMOVE THE BEEF FLANK from the Guinness and leave to dry on kitchen paper. Remove the bacon, bay leaves and thyme and set aside. Put the Guinness in a large saucepan and gently bring to the boil. Skim off the excess foam and pass the Guinness through a fine sieve.

HEAT THE VEGETABLE OIL in a large hot casserole pan and add the carrots, onions, garlic, thyme, bay leaves and the piece of smoked bacon and caramelize well. Put the vegetables into a colander to drain away any excess oil. Coat the beef flank in flour and season generously, seal it in the same pan with a little fresh vegetable oil. Drain away the excess oil, put the vegetables on top of the meat, pour the sieved Guinness over and cook over a high heat to reduce the Guinness by half. Add the veal stock, reboil, skim away the foam and place a sheet of greaseproof paper on top. Cover with a lid and braise in a preheated oven at 140°C/275°F/gas 1 for 2½–3 hours.

REMOVE THE BEEF FLANK from the oven and allow it to cool in the liquor. Once cool, pass the sauce through a fine sieve, then through a muslin cloth. Return to the saucepan and boil. Check the seasoning (remembering that oysters can be quite salty) and reduce. Put the cold flank on a chopping board and cut it into four or more pieces. This will simply need reheating in some hot braising liquor before serving.

SEASON AND SEAL THE BEEF fillet on all sides in a hot ovenproof frying pan with a touch of oil. Roast in a preheated oven at 180°C/350°F/gas 4 for 8–10 minutes. Leave to rest for 10 minutes.

OPEN THE OYSTERS and rinse in a bowl of cold water. Reheat the watercress purée in a pan and reheat the beef fillet in a hot oven. Bring 100 ml of the reduced braising liquor to the boil, add two raw oysters and blend with a hand blender until smooth. Do not reboil. Place the fillets on four plates and spoon over the watercress purée. Arrange the pieces of braised flank on the plates and spoon over the beef and oyster sauce. Set a raw oyster on the side of each plate in a shell.

This dish is full of classic combinations, married together into one fantastic autumnal dish. Cook the beef flank in exactly the same way as in Beef in Guinness with Watercress and Oysters (see page 137), simply using red wine instead of the Guinness.

Beef Fillet with Parsley Risotto, Braised Snails and Red Wine Garlic

SERVES 4
24 cooked snails
100 ml red wine sauce
   (see page 211)
8 heads of garlic
200 ml red wine
200 ml ruby port
3 bunches of picked flat leaf parsley
4 pieces of beef fillet, 130 g each
100 g tempura batter mix
   (available from Asian food stores)
1 kg piece of flank
   (cooked as on page 137)
1 quantity risotto base
   (see page 209)
50 g Parmesan cheese, shaved
caster sugar (optional)
salt and pepper

RINSE THE SNAILS under cold running water and leave to infuse in the red wine sauce.

PEEL FOUR HEADS OF GARLIC and blanch three times in cold water, bringing the water to the boil each time and then refreshing under cold running water. When the garlic is soft, cover it with the red wine and port and heat to reduce until almost dry. Transfer to a blender and blend until smooth. Pass through a fine sieve, check the seasoning and keep warm.

CUT THE TOPS off the remaining heads of garlic and confit them as in the recipe on page 90, caramelizing the garlic with honey as described.

BRING A LARGE SAUCEPAN of salted water to the boil and plunge in all the parsley leaves. Cook for 2–3 minutes in a rapid boil until soft. Use a perforated spoon to remove the parsley from the water. Place in a blender and blend to make a smooth purée. You may need to add a little of the cooking liquor to make it easier to blend. Pass through a fine sieve into a bowl over iced water to chill immediately.

SEASON THE FILLETS with salt, put them into a hot ovenproof frying pan and caramelize well on all sides. Cook in a preheated oven at 180°C/350°F/gas 4 for 8 minutes or until the meat reaches 40°C/100°F inside. Allow the meat to rest for at least 10 minutes on a wire rack.

MAKE UP THE TEMPURA batter according to the packet instructions. Coat 12 of the snails in the batter and deep-fry until golden brown. Season with salt and set aside.

SLICE THE BRAISED FLANK and reheat in the red wine sauce together with the snails. Put the fillets into the oven to reheat. Warm the risotto, stirring in the parsley purée, add the grated Parmesan and season lightly with salt.

SPREAD THE RISOTTO onto the four plates. Spoon the red wine garlic purée onto the plates and sit the garlic confit on the purée. Slice the fillets and arrange the pieces on the plates along with the braised beef. Spoon the red wine sauce over the meats along with the snails and finally scatter over the deep-fried snails and Parmesan shavings.

This is a perfect brasserie dish and a good, light way to enjoy
a piece of roast beef.

Salad of Beef Rib with Truffle Potatoes and Watercress Salad

SERVES 4
12 new potatoes
¼ quantity truffle vinaigrette
  (see page 211)
4 very thin slices of sourdough
  bread
4 rib eye steaks, about 120 g each
vegetable oil
1 quantity watercress purée
  (see page 203)
100 ml red wine sauce
  (see page 211)
50 g fresh cobnuts or hazelnuts,
  blanched and skinned
500 g watercress
4 toasted hazelnuts
salt
cracked black pepper

PUT THE POTATOES in plenty of boiling salted water and cook on a low simmer until they are soft. Leave the potatoes to cool in water and then use a small knife to peel away the skin, trying not to damage the potato. Cut the potatoes into slices 2 cm thick (you need about ten slices per portion) and lay them out on a tray. Top each slice with a generous teaspoon of truffle vinaigrette. Cover the tray with clingfilm and set aside.

LAY THE SLICES of bread on a baking tray and dry them in a preheated oven at 120°C/230°F/gas ½ for about 30 minutes. Break up the bread into small pieces and set aside.

SEASON THE STEAKS generously with salt and cracked black pepper. Heat a large frying pan, add a little vegetable oil to the pan and cook the steaks for about 3 minutes on each side to caramelize. The steaks should now be cooked to medium rare. Transfer the steaks to a wire rack and leave to rest for 5 minutes.

PLACE THE TRUFFLE POTATOES in a steamer to reheat. Reheat the watercress purée in a small pan. Boil the red wine jus, add a couple of teaspoons of the truffle vinaigrette and reboil.

PUT THE TRUFFLE POTATOES on four plates and spoon over the watercress purée. Cut the meat into thin slices and arrange them on plates with the fresh cobnuts or hazelnuts. Scatter watercress over the beef, grate the toasted hazelnuts over the salad, spoon the red wine jus over and arrange the croutons on the plate.

I used to cook venison in a hay box, which is quite a common and old-fashioned way of cooking. Then a Polish friend, Wojciech Modest Amaro, introduced me to the strong and distinctive flavour of bison grass. The venison and chocolate are both strong enough to take on the flavour of the grass. You should be able to purchase bison grass from a good Polish delicatessen.

Venison Baked in Bison Grass with Beetroot, Fig and Bitter Chocolate

SERVES 4
1 large beetroot
14 black figs
½ bottle of red wine
½ bottle of ruby port
juice of 3 lemons
caster sugar (optional)
good handful of fresh bison grass
1 loin of venison, at least 560 g
  (trimmed of all sinew)
vegetable oil
4 sheets of filo
50 ml honey
½ quantity beetroot purée
  (see page 204)
30 g bitter chocolate
  (70 per cent cocoa)
100 ml brown chicken stock
  (see page 199)
salt and pepper

WRAP THE BEETROOT in foil and bake it in a preheated oven at 160°C/310°F/gas 2½ for 1 hour.

MEANWHILE, chop all but four of the figs fairly roughly. Put the pieces in a large saucepan and cover with the red wine and port. Bring to the boil and reduce the liquor by half. Put the reduced liquor in a blender and blend until smooth, season with the lemon juice and some sugar, if needed. Pass through a fine sieve and keep warm.

PUT THE BISON GRASS in a casserole pan, cover and place over a low heat. Season and seal the venison loin all over in hot frying pan with a touch of oil. When the bison grass begins to smoke, add the venison, re-cover and cook in a preheated oven at 180°C/350°F/gas 4 for 8–10 minutes (depending on the thickness of the loin).

UNWRAP THE BEETROOT and peel away the skin. (If you leave it wrapped in foil for 5 minutes after cooking it will sweat slightly, making it easy to rub the skin away.) Cut the beetroot into 2 cm dice.

PREPARE THE FILO as in the recipe on page 46, cutting them into rectangles about 10 x 3 cm. Slice the whole figs (you need four slices from each fig), put them on a tray and drizzle over the honey. Place under a preheated hot grill for 30 seconds or so to soften the figs.

REMOVE THE VENISON from the oven, remove the lid and leave the meat to rest for 10 minutes in the pan.

TO SERVE, reheat the fig purée, the beetroot purée and the chicken stock. Put the diced baked beetroot into the stock and reduce it by half. Spoon the beetroot purée onto four plates. Melt the bitter chocolate into the fig purée. Spoon half the fig purée onto the plates and spread the other half onto the filo tarts. Place four slices of fig on four of the tart bases and top them with the other tart bases to make a sandwich. Cut the venison into thin slices and arrange on the plates. Spoon the jus over the meat.

This dish is unlike me: I'm not usually keen on kidneys and I never cook with curry. I had an Indian sous chef, Binu, for 18 months, and he taught me how to make a good curry. The sauce actually works brilliantly with the kidneys. I cold eat them by the panful like this.

Loin of Lamb with Curried Lambs' Kidneys and Mangoes

SERVES 4
4 lambs' kidneys
1 tablespoon sultanas
25 ml white wine vinegar
2 baby aubergines
olive oil
4 sprigs thyme
2 tablespoons runny honey
2 lamb loins, trimmed of sinew
4 large alfonso mangoes
2 limes
75 ml lamb stock (see page 202)
150 g couscous
2 tablespoons chopped fresh
  coriander
salt

CURRY SAUCE
3 g cumin seeds
3 g coriander seeds
3 g cardamom pods
1 cinnamon stick
vegetable oil
15 g chopped garlic
15 g chopped fresh ginger
2 bay leaves
2 onions, finely chopped
1 tomato, chopped
1 green chilli, sliced in half
50 ml double cream
2 tablespoons chopped fresh
  coriander
1 lime

SPICE MIX
7 g ground chilli
15 g ground coriander
3 g ground cumin
3 g ground garam masala
3 g ground turmeric

FIRST MAKE THE CURRY SAUCE. Fry the cumin, coriander seeds, cardamom and the cinnamon sticks in a little vegetable oil for about 3–4 minutes. Then add the garlic, ginger and bay leaves and cook for a further 2 minutes. Add the chopped onions and cook on a fairly moderate heat until they turn golden brown. Add the spice mix to the onions and cook for a further 2 minutes. Now add the chopped tomato and chilli and cook for a further 4 minutes before adding enough water to just cover the onion and spices. Cook on a low heat until the onions become very soft. Finally add the double cream and the fresh coriander and bring to the boil. Remove the chilli from the sauce and blend until smooth. Pass through a sieve, season with lime juice and a little salt.

PEEL THE SINEW from the outside of the kidneys, cut them in half lengthways and remove any excess lamb fat.

PLACE THE SULTANAS and the vinegar into a small pan and gently bring to the boil, remove from the heat and leave them to cool.

CUT THE AUBERGINES in half lengthways and place them, cut side down, into a hot frying pan with a touch of olive oil and the thyme. Season with salt and caramelize until golden brown. Now add the honey allowing it to fully coat the aubergines. Remove from the heat and set aside.

SEASON THE LAMB LOINS with salt and pepper and place into a warm frying pan, with the fat side facing down. Cook over a low heat and once the skin is nicely caramelized and the majority of the fat is rendered away increase the heat and turn the lamb over, sealing the meat on all sides. Then place the meat into an oven on 180°C/350°F/gas 4 for approx 6 minutes. Use an electronic temperature probe to ensure the core temperature of the meat reaches at least 45°C/100°F. Remove from the oven and allow to rest on a wire rack.

PEEL AND SLICE THE MANGOES and using a small cutter cut out 20 discs of mango. Place the remainder of the mango flesh into a blender with the juice of 1 lime and blend until smooth. Pass through a fine sieve and set aside. Place the mango discs into a hot frying pan with a touch of olive oil and caramelize on all sides. Set aside and keep warm.

HEAT THE LAMB STOCK and add the cooking liquor (honey) from the baby aubergines. Keep warm.

PLACE THE COUSCOUS, the chopped coriander, the pickled sultanas, a touch of salt to season, the zest of 1 lime grated on a microplane into a bowl. Add 150 ml of boiling water and cover with cling film. Leave for at least 5 minutes before removing the cling film and adding the lime juice.

HEAT THE MANGO DISCS, the lamb loin and the baby aubergine in the oven. Spoon the mango purée onto 4 plates along side the couscous. Place a frying pan on the heat and season the kidneys with salt, add a dash of vegetable oil, then fry the lamb's kidneys quickly on one side for about 30 seconds, then again for another 30 seconds on the other side. Now spoon 4–5 tablespoons of the curry sauce into the pan with the kidneys. Remove from the pan and place 2 kidney halves on each plate.

CARVE THE LAMB LOIN thinly and arrange on the plate with the aubergines and the mango discs. Spoon over the lamb sauce.

These two ingredients – new season lamb and Jersey Royals – are at their best at the same time of the year so this seems a natural marriage to me. The flavour of Jersey Royals derives from the unique growing conditions on the island. These potatoes are a true seasonal gem, and around 99 per cent of the crop is exported to the mainland, while the rest are enjoyed by the inhabitants of Jersey. How lucky are we?

Lamb Cutlets with Jersey Royals, Artichoke and Truffle

SERVES 4
2 racks of new season lamb (8 bones, French trimmed and tied)
8 large Jersey Royal potatoes
75 g rock salt
50 g butter
75 g summer truffle, chopped
1 teaspoon picked thyme leaves
2 large globe artichokes
500 ml artichoke cooking liquor (see page 198)
olive oil
20 g butter, diced
100 ml lamb stock (see page 202)
salt and pepper

SEASON THE LAMB with salt and pepper and put the racks in a warm pan, fat side down, and cook very slowly, turning the lamb occasionally. I quite like to cook the lamb on top of the stove because it renders nearly all the fat away, giving a leaner piece of meat. Unfortunately, it takes nearly 45 minutes to cook it like this. If you prefer, roast the lamb in a preheated oven at 180°C/350°F/gas 4 for 8–10 minutes. Allow the meat to rest for at least 10 minutes before you reheat it to serve it.

RINSE THE POTATOES under cold running water to rid them of any soil. Don't scrub away all the skin. Put the rock salt in a baking tray, put the potatoes on top and cook in a preheated oven 180°C/350°F/gas 4 for at least 45 minutes. Allow the potatoes to cool, then cut the tops off and use a teaspoon to scoop the flesh out, taking care not to damage the skins.

PUT THE POTATO in a pan and use a wooden spoon mix in the butter, half the chopped truffle and the thyme leaves. When they are fully incorporated season with salt and pepper, transfer to a piping bag and keep warm.

PREPARE THE ARTICHOKES (see page 80), leave them whole and boil rapidly in the artichoke cooking liquor. Allow the artichokes to cool in the liquor. When they are cool cut them into quarters, put them in a hot frying pan with a little olive and a knob of butter and gently roast until golden brown.

REMOVE THE STRING from the lamb racks and return them to the oven with the potato to reheat.

REHEAT THE LAMB JUS, add the remaining chopped truffle and whisk in the diced butter.

PIPE THE MASHED POTATO into the shells and replace the lids. Cut the lamb into cutlets and arrange them the plates with the potatoes and artichokes. Spoon the lamb jus over the meat and serve.

Always try to buy sweetbreads from around the heart and not the throat, the main difference being that there's a lot more sinew on those from the throat and more texture to those from the heart. These could be served as an accompaniment for a main course or just on their own as a starter.

Lamb Sweetbreads, Tongue and Broad Bean Fricassee

SERVES 4
4 lambs' tongues
1 kg fresh broad beans
1 carrot, peeled and halved
½ onion, peeled
½ head of garlic
200 g fresh lambs' sweetbreads
vegetable oil
100 g girolle mushrooms, cleaned
3 tablespoons shallot confit
   (see page 210)
100 ml lamb stock (see page 202)
knob of butter
2 tablespoons chopped flat leaf
   parsley
salt and pepper

SOAK THE LAMBS' TONGUES in water overnight to help extract the blood.

REMOVE THE BROAD BEANS from their pods and blanch them in plenty of boiling salted water. Refresh immediately in iced water, then remove the skins. Set aside.

PUT THE LAMBS' TONGUES in cold water and bring to the boil. Simmer for 3–4 minutes, remove the tongues and discard the dirty water. Return the tongues to a clean pan, cover with water and add the carrot, onion and garlic. Bring to the boil, skim off any foam and add a handful of salt. Reduce the heat and simmer for 2–3 hours, topping up with fresh water when needed. The lambs' tongues are cooked when you can peel the skin away. Allow them to cool in the liquor. Once cooled, peel the skin off and cut the tongues into bite-sized pieces. Pass the liquor through a fine sieve and store the tongues in the liquor until needed.

BRING A LARGE PAN of water to the boil. Plunge the sweetbreads into the water, bring back to the boil and then immediately plunge the sweetbreads into iced water to stop them from cooking. Once chilled, remove from the iced water and peel away the sinew and fat. This should leave you with nugget-sized pieces of sweetbread.

PAT THE SWEETBREADS dry on a kitchen paper. Heat a large nonstick frying pan, add a touch of vegetable oil and fry the sweetbreads until golden brown and caramelized. Add the mushrooms and shallot confit and cook for a further 2 minutes. Season with salt and pepper, add the broad beans and the lamb stock, bring to the boil, add a knob of butter, reboil, add the chopped parsley and serve.

This is not your everyday loin of lamb recipe. I took quite a bit of flack for this dish from one employer, who said, 'You can't serve lamb with mussels; you have to keep lamb traditional.' If everybody always did the same thing, the world – in my eyes – would be a very boring place. Anyhow, the customers seem to enjoy it and that's what's most important.

Loin of Lamb with Green Olive and Celery Purée, Mussels and Cardamom

SERVES 4
2 whole loins of new season lamb
2 kg mussels
8 celery sticks
2 shallots, chopped
6 split cardamom pods
10 sprigs of thyme
2¹/₂ garlic cloves, coarsely chopped
olive oil
100 ml white wine
100 ml double cream
1 quantity green olive and celery
 purée (see page 204)
3 eggs
50 g dried breadcrumbs
¹/₂ bunch of flat leaf parsley
1 tablespoon picked thyme leaves
100 ml white chicken stock
 (see page 199)
250 g lambs' sweetbreads from
 the heart
100 ml lamb stock (see page 202)
rind and juice of 1 orange
1 tablespoon picked marjoram
 leaves
young leaves from a head of celery
salt and pepper

COOK THE LAMB LOIN as in the recipe on page 144.

CLEAN THE MUSSELS of any beards, put them in a large bowl of cold running water and discard any that float. Heat a large casserole pan over a fierce heat. Coarsely chop four celery sticks and mix them with the chopped shallots, cardamom pods, eight thyme sprigs and two garlic cloves. Drain the mussels thoroughly, add a little olive oil to the hot pan and add the vegetables. Put the mussels on top, add the white wine and cover quickly. Cook the mussels for 3–4 minutes. Remove the lid and drain the liquid into a pan through a fine sieve. Remove the mussels from their shells and store them in a little of the sieved liquor.

REDUCE THE REMAINING liquor by two-thirds, add the cream and reduce again by half. Cover with clingfilm and set aside.

MIX THE GREEN OLIVE and celery purée with the eggs, whisk thoroughly and pass through a fine sieve. Transfer to 8 small rectangular moulds, 5 x 3 cm, lined with clingfilm and foil. Steam at 85°C/185°F for 8 minutes or until the eggs are just set. Keep warm.

PUT THE BREADCRUMBS, parsley, thyme leaves and remaining garlic in a food processor and blend for 4–5 minutes. The breadcrumbs will become bright green and acquire a strong flavour. Pass them through a sieve. Coat eight of the mussels in the green crumbs and set aside. Put the remaining mussels in the cooking liquor cream.

CUT TWO CELERY STICKS into 1 cm dice. Put them in a saucepan with the remaining thyme sprigs. Cover with the stock, season with a little salt and cook slowly for 30 minutes.

PREPARE AND COOK the lambs' sweetbreads as in Lamb Sweetbreads, Tongue and Broad Bean Fricassee (see page 147). Drain them well, heat a small frying pan with a little oil, season the sweetbreads and cook them in the hot oil to caramelize on all sides until golden brown. Reheat the lamb stock. Add the sweetbreads, the diced, braised celery and the picked marjoram leaves.

PLACE THE LAMB LOIN in the oven to reheat. Reheat the custard moulds in the steamer and the mussels in the cream on the stove. Add the orange rind and juice to the mussel cream and reboil. Deep-fry the breadcrumb-coated mussels in a fryer set at 160°C/310°F for 1 minute.

TURN THE CUSTARD moulds out onto the four plates. Carve the lamb, arranging three nuggets on each plate. Spoon the mussel cream around the plate and spoon the lamb jus around the plate. Allow two sweetbreads for each plate. Place them on the deep-fried mussels. Slice the remaining celery stick as finely as possible on a mandolin and dress with the young celery leaves.

This dish doesn't stay on the menu for very long, and the hawthorn flowers don't hang around for very long either but don't worry – it's just as delicious without them. Luckily, they are in bloom long enough to pair with the first batch of St George's mushrooms. Hawthorn has a distinctive, nutty taste, quite like that of hazelnuts. Gloucester Old Spot or Middle White pork would be perfect for this dish or even a rack or roasted leg of a suckling pig.

Pork Chop with Pear, Hawthorn and St George's Mushrooms

SERVES 4
rack of pork (4 bones, French trimmed and tied)
4 pears
juice of 1 lemon
1 teaspoon caster sugar
400 g fresh broad beans
100 g small trimmed St George's mushrooms
50 g butter
3 tablespoons shallot confit (see page 210)
50 ml hazelnut oil
handful of freshly picked hawthorn flowers
100 ml brown chicken stock (see page 199)
4 toasted hazelnuts
salt and pepper

SEASON THE RACK of pork with salt and pepper. Place it, skin side down, in a nonstick, ovenproof frying pan and cook it slowly over a very low heat for up to an hour to render the fat (the more slowly you cook it on the stove the better the crackling will be). Cover the skin with a sheet of foil to stop it from burning. The temperature should be at least 55°C/130°F inside the meat (check with an electric temperature probe). Allow the meat to rest for at least 15 minutes.

PEEL AND CORE THREE PEARS and finely chop the flesh. Place the chopped pear in a pan with half the lemon juice, the sugar and 50 ml water. Cover and cook until the pears are very soft. If there is any water left, remove the lid and reduce the liquid. Transfer the cooked pear to a blender and blend until smooth. Pass through a fine sieve and keep warm.

PEEL AND FINELY SHRED the remaining pear into matchstick size strips, cover with a bit of lemon juice and set aside.

POD THE BROAD BEANS and blanch them in plenty of boiling salted water for 20–30 seconds. Plunge them into a large bowl of iced water to stop them from cooking further. When they are chilled remove them from the water, peel away the skins and set aside.

CLEAN THE MUSHROOMS and put them in a small warm pan over a fairly low heat with a knob of butter and the shallot confit. Cover and sweat the mushrooms until soft. Season with a pinch of salt and some pepper. Add the broad beans, the pear strips, half the hazelnut oil, half the hawthorn flowers and a little lemon juice.

REMOVE THE STRING from the pork rack and return it to the oven to reheat. Heat the chicken jus and add the remaining hazelnut oil, but don't let it boil once you've added the oil.

SPOON THE PEAR PURÉE onto four warm plates. Carve the pork rack and place the slices on the purée. Spoon the mushroom mixture around and spoon the split jus over the rack. Grate the toasted hazelnut over the plate and sprinkle over the remaining hawthorn flowers.

The cooking technique used here lends itself very well to meat from Middle White pigs because the layer of fat under their skin protects the flesh and absorbs the aromatic smoke from the oak bark.

Oak Roast Middle White Pork with Pumpkin Lasagne

SERVES 4
½ large bark pumpkin
½ bunch of sage
300 g chicken mousse
  (see page 214)
finely grated rind and juice
  of 1 lemon
70 g butter
100 g runny honey
1 rack of Middle White pork
  (8 bones, French-trimmed
  and tied)
50 ml vegetable oil
handful of oak bark
150 ml milk
100 g Jabugo ham fat
1 egg, beaten
50 ml béchamel sauce
  (see page 205)
100 ml brown chicken stock
  (see page 199)
150 g grated Manchego cheese
salt and pepper

CUT THE PUMPKIN INTO QUARTERS, peel and finely slice the flesh on a mandolin. Finely dice four of the largest slices, blanch the pieces in boiling salted water until they are just cooked, refresh immediately in iced water, drain and set aside on kitchen paper until needed.

INDIVIDUALLY BLANCH AND REFRESH six more slices of pumpkin, placing them on kitchen paper to dry. Set aside and refrigerate.

FINELY SHRED TEN LEAVES OF SAGE. Fold half the pumpkin dice into the chicken mousse with the shredded sage. Use a microplane or fine grater to grate the lemon rind into the mousse.

LINE A TRAY that is about 4 cm deep and 32 x 24 cm with a double layer of clingfilm. Put a layer of pumpkin slices into the tray, filling all the gaps, then spoon the chicken mousse over the slices and level it with a palette knife. Cover the mousse with another layer of the sliced pumpkin and wrap with the excess clingfilm. Cook in a steamer and for 20–25 minutes until the mousse is firm, then immediately transfer to the refrigerator for at least 3 hours or until the mousse is completely chilled.

FINELY CHOP THE REMAINING THE PUMPKIN SLICES. Melt 50 g butter in a large saucepan, add the chopped pumpkin and remaining sage leaves and season generously with salt. Stir thoroughly, cover and cook over a fairly fast heat, stirring occasionally so that it does not caramelize. It should take about 15 minutes to become soft. When the pumpkin is soft, remove the lid and add the honey. Stir to mix and continue to cook until the liquid is reduced. Transfer to a blender and blend until smooth. Pass through a fine sieve and season with a little lemon juice. Put into a gas canister and charge with a cartridge. Keep warm by standing the canister in a pan of warm water.

SEAL THE PORK ON ALL SIDES in a hot pan with the vegetable oil and 10 g butter and season with salt and pepper. Put the bark in a cast iron casserole pan with a tight-fitting lid and put over a high heat. Place the sealed pork rack in the pan with all the stalks from the sage, cover and allow the bark to smoke for 1–2 minutes. Transfer to a preheated oven at 180°C/350°F/gas 4 and for 18 minutes. Leave the meat to rest in the pan with the lid still in place for at least 10 minutes.

PUT THE MILK IN A SAUCEPAN and heat with the ham fat and five sage leaves. Transfer to a blender, add the Manchego cheese and blend until smooth. Pass the liquid through a fine sieve. Cool and mix in the egg, pass again through a fine sieve and pour the mixture into four jars. Put the lids on the jars and cook them in a steamer for 10 minutes. The sage milk will set like custard.

TURN THE LASAGNE OUT onto a chopping board and remove the clingfilm. Cut the lasagne into pieces about 12 x 8 cm, spoon the béchamel sauce over and reheat in the steamer. Then place under a preheated hot grill to gratinate the béchamel.

REMOVE THE STRING FROM THE PORK, put it back in the oven to reheat and then cut into four portions. Arrange the meat on four plates with the lasagne beside it. Heat the chicken jus, whisk in 10 g butter and add the remaining pumpkin dice. Pour the jus over the lasagne and meat and squirt the warm pumpkin foam on top of the custards.

I use this pork recipe in all different shapes and forms – as a simple pâté to spread on toast or rolled into balls and dipped in tempura batter and deep-fried. This is a recipe that will benefit from being made well in advance.

Pork Rillette with Apple

SERVES 12
2 kg skinless, boneless pork belly
1 bottle of white wine
1 head of garlic, cut in half
   widthways
15 juniper berries, crushed
8 bay leaves
6 Granny Smith apples
salt

CUT THE PORK BELLY into 8 cm dice and put them in a large casserole pan with 3 litres water and the wine, garlic, juniper berries, bay leaves and a couple of tablespoons of salt. Bring to the boil, cover with a sheet of greaseproof paper and a tight-fitting lid and cook in a preheated oven at 130°C/250°F/gas ½ for at least 3 hours.

REMOVE FROM THE OVEN. The pork should be very soft at this stage. If there is any liquid left, bring it back to the boil and reduce slowly. Once all the liquid has evaporated, drain away half the excess fat and set it aside. Remove the bay leaves and the garlic skin.

PEEL THE APPLES and cut them into 1 cm dice.

ALLOW THE PORK BELLY to cool a little, put it in a food processor with a paddle attachment and gently beat until it breaks up. While the meat is in the machine add the diced apple, check the seasoning and add a little more of the fat if the meat is too dry.

TO STORE THE RILLETTE in the long term transfer it to small, sterilized, sealable jars, leaving a small area on top to pour in a layer of the reserved fat. Leave to cool, seal and keep in the refrigerator for up to 3 months if the seal is not broken.

Desserts

Rosemary is one of the most traditional of English herbs, so combining it with a very English fruit seems a natural thing to do.

Apple and Rosemary Mousse with Calvados Ice Cream

SERVES 4
1 quantity Calvados ice cream
  (see page 217)

APPLE CRISPS
125 g caster sugar
juice of 1 lemon
2 Granny Smith apples
2 leaves gelatine, softened

APPLE AND ROSEMARY MOUSSE
5 Granny Smith apples, peeled
  and finely chopped
juice of 1 lemon
100 ml milk
200 ml double cream
3 sprigs of rosemary
6 egg yolks
310 g caster sugar
40 g cornflour
2 gelatine leaves, softened
50 ml calvados
6 egg whites

MAKE THE APPLE CRISPS. Put the sugar and 125 ml water in a saucepan and boil for a couple of minutes. Add the lemon juice. Slice the apples very thinly widthways with a mandolin and put the slices in the hot syrup. Leave them in the liquor to cool for 24 hours. Drain the slices and transfer them to an ovenproof rubber mat and leave them in a preheated oven at no more than 100°C/200°F/gas ¼ overnight. By morning the crisps will still be white and very crisp.

MAKE THE MOUSSE. Put the apples in a saucepan with the lemon juice and a couple of tablespoons of water. Cover and cook over a high heat until the apples are extremely soft and all the liquid has evaporated. Transfer to a blender and blend until smooth, then pass through a fine sieve and set aside.

PUT THE MILK, CREAM AND ROSEMARY in a large saucepan. Bring to a low boil and simmer for a couple of minutes. Set aside and leave to infuse.

MEANWHILE, WHISK THE EGG YOLKS, 210 g sugar and the cornflour to a firm sabayon stage. Gently poor the infused rosemary cream over the egg mixture, mix well and pour back into the pan. Return to the heat and allow the liquid to come to its first bubble (boil), then remove from the heat. While the mixture is still warm, add the gelatine and leave to cool for 15 minutes. Add 300 g of the apple purée and the calvados. Allow the mixture to set in a large bowl over iced water.

BOIL THE REMAINING SUGAR and 50 ml water to 117°C/225°F and, in a separate bowl, whisk the egg whites to a firm peak. Slowly add the boiled sugar to the egg whites and whisk until the mixture has cooled. Fold the meringue into the remaining apple purée and allow to set in the refrigerator.

SPOON THE MOUSSE into four chilled bowls with the calvados ice cream and serve with apple crisps.

This is a perfect winter dessert, reminiscent of a classic tarte tatin.
It's really very easy and makes a great Sunday lunch dessert.

Baby Pear and Ginger Tart

SERVES 4
200 g caster sugar
125 g unsalted butter, diced
50 g candied ginger, finely chopped
2 x 400 g cans baby pears, drained
1 sheet of puff pastry, rolled out to
 a circle 30 cm across
10 g sugar
1 quantity candied ginger ice cream
 (see page 217)

MAKE A CARAMEL by boiling 50 ml water with the 200 g sugar until
it reaches a dark golden colour. Slowly add the butter, whisking
continuously, then pour the caramel into a 30 cm nonstick, ovenproof
frying pan and allow it to cool slightly.

SPRINKLE THE CANDIED ginger over the caramel. Arrange the baby
pears around the pan, cover with the puff pastry and press down the
pastry around the pears to give a snug fit. Sprinkle 10 g sugar over
the pastry and bake in a preheated oven at 210°C/420°F/gas 6 for
20 minutes. Reduce the heat to 170°C/325°F/gas 3 and cook for a
further 10 minutes.

ALLOW THE TART to sit for 5 minutes and then place a plate that is the
same size as the pan over the pan and, very carefully, flip the pan over –
making sure that you hold the plate in place. The tart will be beautifully
caramelized and ready for you to slice and serve with the candied
ginger ice cream.

You need a total of 13 Granny Smith apples for this recipe. I love using the same ingredient in different ways and experimenting with different textures. Here you have a sweet, buttery apple terrine alongside a sharp and refreshing apple sorbet and a creamy cinnamon mousse.

Baked Apple Terrine with Cinnamon Mousse and Green Apple Sorbet

SERVES 4
1 quantity green apple sorbet
  (see page 218)

PRESSED APPLE TERRINE
10 Granny Smith apples
200 g unsalted butter, melted
200 g demerara sugar
2 tablespoons ground cinnamon
4 tablespoons lemon thyme leaves

CINNAMON MOUSSE
200 ml crème anglaise
  (see page 216)
1 teaspoon ground cinnamon
2 leaves gelatine, softened
200 ml double cream, semi-
  whipped

APPLE JELLY
2 Granny Smith apples
3 leaves gelatine, softened
75 g caster sugar
juice of 1 lemon

CARAMELIZED APPLE DICE
1 Granny Smith apple, peeled
  and finely diced
100 g caster sugar
25 g unsalted butter
50 ml calvados

MAKE THE APPLE TERRINE. Butter a small rectangular baking tray and line it with greaseproof paper. Slice the apples as thinly as possible, preferably using a mandolin. Place a layer of apple slices over the bottom of the baking tray and brush with melted butter. Sprinkle over a thin layer of sugar, a pinch of cinnamon and a few lemon thyme leaves. Continue layering until all the apples are used or you have reached the top of the tray. Cover with a sheet of greaseproof paper and cook in a preheated oven at 160°C/310°F/gas 2½ for 35 minutes. Check that the apples are cooked by inserting the tip of a small knife; if the crunch has disappeared the terrine is ready. When you remove the terrine from the oven sit it on another tray to catch any of the excess juices that may escape. Place another baking tray (the same size as the one the terrine is in) on top of the terrine and apply some pressure, such as small tins, to help the terrine press. Transfer the terrine to the refrigerator, with the weights still in place.

MAKE THE APPLE JELLY. Pass the apples through a vegetable juicer. Transfer the juice to a saucepan, bring to the boil and pass immediately through a muslin cloth into a bowl set over iced water. Place a small amount of the apple juice into a small pan and return to the heat. Add the gelatine and dissolve. When the gelatine has dissolved add the heated apple juice back to the cold juice. Mix well. Pour the semi-set apple jelly into stainless steel moulds lined with clingfilm. Transfer to the refrigerator until fully set, which will take a couple of hours. Spoon the remaining apple jelly into a pressurized gas canister and charge with two gas cartridges. Keep in the refrigerator.

MAKE THE CINNAMON MOUSSE. Warm the crème anglaise slightly, and mix in the ground cinnamon and gelatine. When the gelatine has melted pass the mixture through a fine sieve into a bowl set over iced water. Place half into the stainless steel moulds (on top of the apple jelly). Leave the other half to set, then fold in the cream, transfer the mixture to a piping bag and keep refrigerated until you need it.

MAKE THE CARAMELIZED APPLE DICE. Put the apple pieces in a hot frying pan and sprinkle over the sugar. When the apple begins to

caramelize add the butter. As soon as the butter begins to foam add the calvados – the butter and alcohol will emulsify. Remove to a tray and spread out the mixture so that it stops cooking.

TO SERVE, remove the greaseproof paper from the top of the terrine, turn it out onto a chopping board and cut four slices with a long slicing knife. Arrange them on plates and decorate with the caramelized apple. Turn out the jellies onto the plates and pipe cinnamon mousse next to them. Spoon the apple sorbet next to the jelly. Finally squirt a small amount of apple mousse from the canister next to the terrine.

This dish was inspired by my favourite cocktail, the Bramble, invented by the amazing bartender Dick Bradsell. You should start preparing the recipe the day before you want to serve it.

Iced Blackberry and Apple Parfait with Gin Sabayon and Warm Pancakes

SERVES 4

BLACKBERRY PARFAIT
450 g blackberries
175 caster sugar
2–3 tablespoons crème de cassis
6 egg yolks
350 ml cream, semi-whipped
2 Granny Smith apples,
   finely diced

GIN SABAYON
3 egg yolks
125 g icing sugar
20 ml gin
150 ml double cream,
   semi-whipped
200 ml cold milk

PANCAKES
2 eggs
50 g caster sugar
150 g plain flour
10 g baking powder
100 ml cold milk
vegetable oil

MAKE THE PARFAIT. Put the blackberries, 75 g sugar and the crème de cassis in a saucepan. Cover and cook over a low heat for about 5 minutes until the blackberries give up their natural juices. Remove the pan from the heat and leave to cool at room temperature. Dissolve the remaining sugar in a saucepan with 4 tablespoons water over a low heat. Increase the heat and bring the liquid to 117°C/225°F. Meanwhile, use an electric beater to whisk the yolks until they have doubled in volume and are light in colour. While the machine is still running, gently pour the sugar mixture over the eggs. Continue to whisk until the mixture is cool. Fold in the cream, half the blackberries (reserving the remainder for serving) and the finely diced apple. Pour the mixture into a tray lined with greaseproof paper and freeze overnight.

MAKE THE SABAYON. In a round-bottomed stainless steel bowl mix together the egg yolks, icing sugar and gin. Sit over a pan of boiling water and whisk until the sabayon becomes light and firm. Take care that it does not become too hot or the egg mixture will scramble. Transfer the cooked mixture to a bowl over iced water and whisk until chilled. Then fold in the cream and refrigerate until needed.

MAKE THE PANCAKES. Whisk together the eggs and sugar. Fold in the flour and baking powder and gradually add the milk, whisking vigorously to avoid any lumps. Heat a large nonstick frying pan, add a dash of vegetable oil and spoon the mixture into the pan to make four pancakes. Cook for a minute or so and then use a palette knife to turn the pancakes over, and cook them very briefly on the other side. Remove from the pan to some kitchen paper.

TO SERVE, place a pancake on each plate, spoon the remaining blackberries on to the pancakes. Coat the blackberries with the gin sabayon and glaze with a blowtorch. Slice the frozen parfait and serve next to the pancakes.

This is a fairly simple recipe, which is all the better if you wait until black figs come into season. Some fig trees produce fruit twice a year, with harvests in early July and then in August/September, so you don't have to wait too long for them to come round again. The chocolate tuile recipe is a useful one to keep in the freezer for future use, so divide this mixture into four batches and freeze three of them.

Fig and Filo Tart with Burnt Honey Ice Cream and Caramelized Chocolate Tuile

SERVES 4
1 quantity burnt honey ice cream
  (see page 216)
4 black figs
100 ml honey

FIG PURÉE
10 black figs, quartered
1/2 bottle red wine
1/2 bottle ruby port
100 ml lemon juice
50 g caster sugar

CHOCOLATE TUILES
155 g unsalted butter
95 g glucose
285 g caster sugar
4 g pectin
25 g cocoa powder
85 g chocolate (64 per cent)

FILO TART
8 black figs
100 g caster sugar
3 sheets of filo pastry
1 tablespoon cinnamon

MAKE THE BURNT honey ice cream and store it in the freezer until needed.

MAKE THE FIG PURÉE. Put the fig quarters into a large saucepan, cover with the wine and port and bring to the boil. Allow to simmer until the liquid has evaporated. Transfer to a blender and blend until smooth. Pass through a fine sieve and add the lemon juice and sugar. Mix thoroughly, cover with clingfilm and refrigerate.

MAKE THE TUILE. Melt the butter and glucose in a small pan, add the sugar and pectin and mix well. Dissolve the cocoa powder in 85 ml warm water and then melt the chocolate in the cocoa powder liquid. Add this to the sugar mixture. Mix together thoroughly, then pour the mixture onto a baking tray lined with greaseproof paper. Cook in a preheated oven at 180°C/350°F/gas 4 until small bubbles appear in the centre. (The bubbles will be quite large at first, but will then become small.) Remove the tray from the oven, place another sheet of greaseproof on top and use a rolling pin to remove the tuile mixture. Be careful because it is very hot. Peel the paper from the top and while the mixture is still slightly warm cut it to your desired shape. The tuiles will quickly become crisp, and you can pop them in and out of the oven to soften them slightly.

PREPARE THE FILO PASTRY. You will need two baking trays the same size. Cut the eight figs into five slices. Put the sugar in a saucepan with 50 ml water and simmer for 5 minutes. Allow to cool slightly. Put a piece of greaseproof paper on the underneath of one of the baking trays and lay a sheet of filo pastry on top. Use a pastry brush to apply a coat of syrup to the pastry, then liberally scatter slices of fig on top of the filo. Dust with half the cinnamon powder. Lay another sheet of filo on top and repeat the process, placing the sliced figs in different places from those in the first layer. Lay the final sheet of filo on top and again brush with the syrup. Put a sheet of greaseproof on top of the final layer of pastry, then place the second baking tray on top. (The bottoms of two trays should be facing each other.) Place a weight on the top tray and cook the filo tart in a preheated oven at 160°C/310°F/gas 2½ for 15–20 minutes.

REMOVE THE TART from the oven and remove the top tray and sheet
of greaseproof paper. While the tart is still warm cut it into rectangles
about 12 x 4 cm (you need at least eight pieces). Cover again with
greaseproof paper and return to the oven with the second tray on top.
Cook for a further 5 minutes. They should be slightly crisp. Remove
from the oven and transfer to a wire rack to cool.

CUT THE REMAINING four figs into three slices and place them on
a baking tray. Drizzle over the honey and place under a preheated
hot grill until the figs are soft and the honey begins to bubble.

TO SERVE, spoon some fig purée on to four plates and spread more
purée on to all the filo rectangles (any unused purée can be frozen for
use later). Lay three slices of fig on four of the rectangles and top with
the remaining four filo slices to form a 'sandwich'. Place a fig and filo
tart on each of the plates, spoon on the burnt honey ice cream and
rest the chocolate tuile on the ice cream.

The flavour combinations in this dish may seem unusual but they really do work. Never be afraid to experiment. You will need to start this recipe the day before you want to serve it.

Iced Pistachio Parfait, Basil Jelly, Parmesan Ice Cream and Black Olive Tuiles

SERVES 4
1 quantity crème anglaise
  (see page 216)
30 g Parmesan cheese,
  very finely grated
pistachio nuts, chopped, to serve

BLACK OLIVE TUILES
30 g unsalted butter, melted
100 g demerara sugar
50 g egg whites
50 g plain flour
50 g black olive purée

ICED PISTACHIO PARFAIT
250 ml milk
200 g caster sugar
8 egg yolks
2 leaves gelatine, softened
150 g pistachio paste
50 g peeled pistachios, chopped
400 ml double cream, semi-
  whipped

BASIL JELLY
300 g basil leaves
2 leaves gelatine, softened
50 g caster sugar

PISTACHIO AND CARAMEL CRISP
100 g caster sugar
30 g glucose
50 g peeled pistachios, chopped

MAKE THE TUILES by mixing together all the ingredients. Transfer to a piping bag and leave in the refrigerator overnight. Put an ovenproof rubber mat on a baking tray, pipe the mixture the length of the tray and cook in a preheated oven at 180°C/350°F/gas 4 for 10 minutes. While the mixture is still warm, roll into spirals. Leave to go cold and crisp.

PREPARE THE CRÈME anglaise and add the finely grated Parmesan while still warm. Leave to infuse for 1 hour and then pass again through a fine sieve. Churn in an ice cream machine and freeze until needed.

MAKE THE PISTACHIO parfait. Boil the milk with half the sugar. Mix together the egg yolks and the remaining sugar and carefully whisk the boiling milk into the egg mixture. Combine thoroughly. Return the mixture to the saucepan, bring back to the boil and add the gelatine and the pistachio paste. Pass through a fine sieve and add the chopped pistachios. Chill in a stainless steel bowl placed over iced water. Before the mixture has fully set, fold in the cream. Pour into a tray lined with clingfilm and freeze for at least 3 hours.

MAKE THE BASIL JELLY. Blanch the basil leaves in a large pan of boiling water until they are soft. Drain the leaves and blend until smooth. While the machine is still running add the gelatine and sugar. Pour the mixture into a bowl that is sitting on iced water. Taste and add more sugar if necessary. Pour the mixture into cylinder moulds, 6 cm across and 1 cm deep. and refrigerate for a couple of hours until fully set.

MAKE THE PISTACHIO and caramel crisp. Cover a stainless steel tray with a fine layer of vegetable oil. At the same time, grease a cylinder mould, about 12 cm across, which will also be used to cut the parfait. Stand the greased moulds on a baking tray. Boil the sugar and glucose with 40 ml water to 156°C/310°F, carefully add the pistachios and pour a very thin layer of the mixture into the moulds. Leave to set until they are crisp. They should be easy to remove from greased tray.

CUT OUT FOUR PARFAITS with the same cylinder mould and place onto four chilled plates. Place a caramel crisp on the parfait, turn the basil jelly out onto the plates and spoon the Parmesan ice cream over the jelly. Finally, add a black olive tuile and some chopped pistachio nuts.

THE PATISSERIE SECTION

More often than not behind every great chef there is a fantastic pastry chef, one cannot live without the other. The excitement of bringing all the elements together when you are planning your desserts takes attention to detail, perfect timing and hard graft and I have been fortunate to have met and worked with some incredible pastry chefs and am in total admiration of their dedication to perfection.

More often than not, the pastry chef is the unsung hero of the professional kitchen. In the restaurant the main dish may be the star of the show but for me, a fantastic meal has to start with a delicious piece of freshly made bread and should end with a glorious dessert. For this reason, a good pastry chef is essential. They are often the first in, making sure the bread is under way, and the last out, only leaving when the final customer has put down their spoon or tried some of the delicious petits fours on offer.

Sophie Gaxette and Kim Holtby are two amazing pastry chefs who are currently working alongside me at The Dorchester Hotel, Park Lane. They both share my excitement of bringing all the elements together. Producing their standard of work requires perfect timing, attention to detail, dedication and a hunger for success; they are constantly looking at new ways of enhancing and improving our ideas and techniques.

We are very reliant on the amazing seasonal fruits that are available in Britain and we look forward with anticipation as the season changes so our menu alters to incorporate the new crop of fruits. There is nothing better than working with a fruit or vegetable when it is in its prime and grown in ideal conditions.

We rejoice particularly when the summer fruits and berries become abundant in June, July and August and in the winter months we rely heavily on apples, pears, blackberries, nuts and chocolate. I also include a very small number of fruit grown outside Europe that we can't live without – banana, pomegranates and passion fruit – and I suggest that these are enjoyed in moderation, when British fruit is relatively sparse

I do, however, think it's a bit silly to buy apples shipped from New Zealand and strawberries from Holland, when for many weeks or months of the year you can feast on far superior native versions – often at a lower cost financially as well as environmentally.

Disciplining yourself to use seasonal fruits can expand your understanding of each variety and often inspires us with new dessert ideas.

The challenges that you have to overcome in the pastry section are completely different to working in other parts of the kitchen. Temperatures, weights and textures all need to be perfect before a dessert becomes a success. Advanced preparation for a successful dessert is essential. To bring all the elements together when we are plating desserts takes serious commitment, precision, timing and a creative spark.

The desserts that I have included in this book are my personal favourites, as well as dishes that have been popular in the restaurant. Some of them may appear quite complex but this is really because I can't resist the temptation to create desserts that combine several different elements. I love pairing a rich sponge dessert with a homemade yogurt or a refreshing sorbet and you will find plenty of basic recipes for ice creams and sorbets in the final chapter of the book. Many of the desserts can be adapted to suit your own tastes or simplified if time is an issue. The vanilla macaroons with lemon purée on page 177 are a perfect accompaniment to the poached rhubarb and yogurt but are also delicious on their own as an afternoon treat. The same applies to many of the cakes and sponges in the book.

One of the other things you will notice is my use of a pressurized gas canister to create foams and mousses. This kitchen gadget can turn a cream into a mousse or a jelly into a foam but if you don't have one, don't worry. The flavours are exactly the same – it is simply the texture that changes.

I love the combination of pineapple and fennel. It is unusual but extremely versatile and lends itself to both sweet and savoury dishes. As well as using it in this dessert, these two ingredients are combined with foie gras earlier in this book to make a starter I often use to kick off a tasting menu (see Roasted Foie Gras with Fennel and Caramelized Pineapple, page 110). You will need to start this recipe a day in advance.

Yogurt Jelly with Roasted Pineapple and Fennel Foam

SERVES 4
1 quantity yogurt sorbet
  (see page 219)
1 quantity homemade yogurt
  (see page 177)

DRIED FENNEL CRISPS
1 fennel bulb
75 ml lemon juice
75 g caster sugar
3 whole star anise

FENNEL FOAM
500 g fennel
100 g caster sugar
2 star anise
4 sprigs of tarragon
100 ml Pernod
juice of 6 lemons
6 leaves gelatine, softened

ROASTED PINEAPPLE
1½ pineapples
1 tablespoons ground star anise
50 g caster sugar
100 ml Pernod

PINEAPPLE JELLY
225 g caster sugar
juice of 1 lemon
4 leaves gelatine, softened

MAKE THE YOGURT SORBET and keep it in the freezer until needed. Make the homemade yogurt and set it in four fairly shallow bowls.

MAKE THE FENNEL CRISPS. Slice the fennel on a gravity slicer or as thinly as possible by hand. Heat together the lemon juice, sugar and the star anise in 250 ml water and simmer for 10 minutes. Add the fennel slices and leave overnight. Remove the fennel from the syrup and spread the slices out on an ovenproof rubber mat on top of a baking tray and leave in a preheated oven at 100°C/200°F/gas ¼ for 4–6 hours. Remove from the oven and allow to cool. Keep the fennel crisps in a dark, dry place in a sealed container until needed.

MAKE THE FENNEL FOAM. Feed the fennel through a juicer, pour the liquid into a saucepan and bring to the boil. Pass through a fine sieve, add the sugar, star anise and tarragon. Return to the heat for 2 more minutes and leave to infuse for 30 minutes. Add the Pernod, lemon juice and gelatine. Pass through a fine sieve again and then leave to set in the refrigerator for at least 4 hours. Spoon the jelly into a gas canister and charge with two cartridges. Shake the bottle for a minute or so and transfer to the refrigerator until needed.

MAKE THE ROASTED PINEAPPLE. Cut twelve 3 cm cubes from the pineapple, reserving the rest for the pineapple jelly. Coat them in the ground star anise and sugar. Put them in a dry, ovenproof frying pan and cook over a medium heat until the cubes have caramelized on all sides. Deglaze the pan with the Pernod and cook in a preheated oven at 160°C/310°F/gas 2½ for 10 minutes.

MAKE THE PINEAPPLE JELLY. Pass the remaining pineapple and all the trimmings through a juicer. Pour the juice into a pan and bring to the boil. Pass through a fine sieve, add the sugar and lemon juice and while the juice is still warm add the gelatine. Pass through a fine sieve again into a bowl over iced water. When the jelly is semi-set, spoon it onto the set yogurt and transfer to the refrigerator to set completely.

WHEN THE PINEAPPLE jelly is set spoon the yogurt sorbet onto the jelly, place the fennel crisps in the sorbet and the roasted pineapple on the jelly. Squirt some fennel foam onto the side of the filled bowls.

Pumpkin is a wonderfully versatile vegetable that is also great in desserts – think of the popular American dessert pumpkin pie. Here the sweetness of the pumpkin is counterbalanced by the tartness of the lemon and the fresh texture of the fromage blanc mousse. You should start preparing this recipe at least 12 hours before you want to serve it.

Fromage Blanc Mousse with Pumpkin Custard and Lemon Verbena Ice Cream

SERVES 4
1 quantity crème anglaise
  (see page 216)
20 lemon verbena leaves
½ bark pumpkin
100 ml honey
juice of 2 lemons
3 eggs
250 g fromage blanc
4 leaves gelatine, softened
50 g caster sugar

INFUSE THE CRÈME ANGLAISE with the lemon verbena leaves at least 12 hours in advance. Remove the verbena and then churn in an ice cream machine. Freeze until needed.

PEEL THE PUMPKIN carefully with a serrated pastry knife. Remove the seeds, chop the flesh as finely as possible and put the pieces in a large heatproof casserole pan with the honey and half the lemon juice. Cover and cook for 20 minutes over a medium heat (do not allow to the pumpkin to colour). Once the pumpkin is cooked, transfer to a blender and blend until smooth. Pass the mixture through a fine sieve and allow to cool.

WHISK THE EGGS into 450 g of the pumpkin purée and pass again through a fine sieve. Taste and if necessary, add a touch of sugar or lemon juice, depending on how sweet your tooth is.

MAKE THE CASINGS. Line four rectangle moulds, each about 11 cm long and 8 cm wide, with clingfilm and foil. Pour the mixture into the moulds so that each is about half full. Put the moulds on a tray, cover with clingfilm and place in a steamer, set at 90°C/190°F, until the mixture is firm and cooked (this should take about 12 minutes). Allow to cool in the refrigerator.

MEANWHILE, soften the fromage blanc in a large bowl and add the rest of the lemon juice. Heat the gelatine gently with 4 tablespoons of water to melt it and add the sugar. Pour this mixture into the fromage blanc and mix thoroughly.

POUR THE FROMAGE blanc mixture onto the chilled pumpkin and leave to set for at least a couple of hours in the refrigerator. When the moulds are fully chilled peel away the clingfilm and foil and run a small warm knife around the inside of the moulds to release the custards. Set these in the centre of the plates and spoon the ice cream over the top.

Strictly speaking, rhubarb is a vegetable because it doesn't contain seeds. Early rhubarb has long, pale pink stems with small leaves and all the freshness and flavour needed to make delicious pies, fools, sorbets or ice creams. Forced or early rhubarb needs very brief cooking and, unless you have a palate for tartness, it always needs sweetening with sugar.

Poached Rhubarb with Vanilla Macaroons and Homemade Yogurt

SERVES 4
½ **quantity lemon purée**
  (see page 203)

HOMEMADE YOGURT
500 ml milk
500 ml double cream
125 g caster sugar
2 vanilla pods
2 g yogurt yeast

POACHED RHUBARB
4 sticks rhubarb
125 g sugar
250 ml water
rind of 1 lemon
1 vanilla pod, split

RHUBARB JELLY
40 ml lemon juice
1 tablespoon caster sugar
4 leaves gelatine, softened
250 g rhubarb poaching liquor

VANILLA MACAROONS
7 egg whites
165 g caster sugar
325 g icing sugar
200 g ground almonds

MAKE THE YOGURT by heating together the milk, cream, sugar and vanilla pods to 90°C/190°F. Allow to cool to 45°C/100°F, remove the vanilla pods, then pour the mixture over the yeast. Mix thoroughly and pour the mixture into four serving bowls. Cover the yogurt with clingfilm and leave to stand in a warm place for 3 hours. When the yogurt has set it can be transferred to the refrigerator.

PREPARE THE RHUBARB. Peel the sticks and cut the flesh into thin strips, about 7 cm long. Put the sugar, vanilla and lemon rind in a saucepan with 250 ml water, bring to the boil and then add the rhubarb strips. Simmer for no more than 2 minutes, then allow the syrup to cool with the rhubarb still resting in it. Reserve 250 ml of the poaching liquor to make the jelly.

MAKE THE JELLY. Put the lemon juice and sugar in a saucepan and heat gently. Add the gelatine and stir until it has dissolved. Add the reserved poaching liquor, mix together, then chill over iced water. When the jelly has begun to set, spoon it over the bowls of yogurt to form a clear layer of jelly. Transfer them to the refrigerator for at least 1 hour to set.

MAKE THE MACAROONS. Whip together the egg whites and sugar to a firm meringue. Mix together the icing sugar and ground almonds, and then fold them into the meringue mixture. Fill a piping bag with the mixture and line a baking tray with greaseproof paper (securely fixing the paper to the tray with a bit of the meringue mixture in each corner). Pipe small amounts of the meringue mixture evenly on the tray. You will need a minimum of 16 macaroons, but the mixture will give you a lot more (any extra macaroons can be stored in an airtight container for up to two weeks). Put them to one side until a skin forms on the macaroons (this should take about 10 minutes), then cook in a preheated oven at 150°C/300°F/gas 2 for 10 minutes.

TO SERVE, arrange the poached rhubarb on top of the jelly, and sandwich the macaroons with the lemon purée.

This is an elegant way to serve a crumble, and the peanuts and the palm sugar are a fantastic combination. You can make the crumble and the peanut tuiles the day before.

Banana and Peanut Crumble with Roasted Pineapple

SERVES 4
1 quantity palm sugar ice cream
   (see page 217)
2 bananas
caster sugar, to coat
$1/2$ pineapple
1 tablespoon ground cinnamon
1 tablespoon ground star anise
50 g caster sugar
50 g unsalted butter
150 ml Malibu

PEANUT CRUMBLE
150 g peanuts, crushed
100 g plain flour
150 g demerara sugar
150 g unsalted butter, diced

PEANUT TUILES
200 g ready-made fondant icing
100 g glucose
100 g isomalt (available from cake
   decorating suppliers)
40 g smooth peanut butter

MAKE THE PEANUT TUILES. Put all the ingredients in a saucepan, mix together and heat, stirring. Allow to cool. Lay an ovenproof rubber mat on a baking tray and spread out the mixture, fairly thinly, forming it into four individual portions. Bake in a preheated oven at 160°C/310°F/gas $2^{1}/2$ for 10–12 minutes until the mixture begins to bubble. Remove from the oven, allow to sit for a minute to cool slightly and then fold the tuiles over a rolling pin to form a cylinder. Leave to cool completely.

MAKE THE CRUMBLE. Toast the crushed peanuts and mix them with the flour and demerara sugar. Using the tips of your fingers, gently work the butter into the dry mixture. The mixture will become quite crumbly. Pour it out onto a tray and bake in a preheated oven at 160°C/310°F/gas $2^{1}/2$ for 15 minutes. Allow to cool then break up the mixture into crumbs with your fingertips.

PEEL THE BANANAS and cut them in half. Square the bananas off, coat them in a little sugar and transfer them to a dry, ovenproof frying pan over a medium heat – the bananas will gradually begin to caramelize. Once they are caramelized on all sides spoon over the crumble and cook in a preheated oven at 160°C/310°F/gas $2^{1}/2$ for 10 minutes.

MEANWHILE, cut the pineapple into 3 cm cubes and coat them in the ground cinnamon and star anise. Put them in a dry frying pan and caramelize slowly on all sides. When the pineapple is fully caramelized, add 50 g sugar, the Malibu and butter and continue to cook until the liquid has reduced to a syrup.

TO SERVE, transfer the caramelized pineapple to four plates, along with the banana crumble. Place a peanut tuile on each plate and carefully spoon ice cream into each tuile. Drizzle the syrup from the pineapple around the plate.

You will need to start this recipe the day before you want to serve it and have four glasses stored in your freezer. Adding a touch of black pepper to the strawberries adds a little bit of heat to this otherwise cooling dessert. My wife, Miranda, prepared a version of this dish for me soon after we first met.

Strawberries with Whisky Granite

SERVES 4
100 g of sugar
juice of 2 limes
300 ml good whisky
100 ml water
200 g strawberries, hulled
clear honey and cracked black
  pepper, to serve

BOIL THE SUGAR and lime juice with 100 ml water. Chill the syrup slightly, then add the whisky. Chill completely, transfer to a stainless steel tray and place in the bottom of the freezer. Leave for at least 12 hours. When the granite is frozen scrape it away from the tray with a fork, put it into a freezer-proof container and return to the freezer until you are ready to serve it. The granite should resemble frozen flakes.

DICE THE STRAWBERRIES and put them into the four frozen glasses. Grind a little cracked black pepper over the strawberries and drizzle with honey. Spoon over the granite and serve.

The flavours of chocolate and lime work beautifully together and the creamy, sweet candied ginger ice cream gives a wonderful extra kick.

Chocolate and Lime Savarin with Candied Ginger Ice Cream

SERVES 4
1 quantity candied ginger ice cream
(see page 217)

CHOCOLATE SAVARIN
75 ml milk
10 g yeast
250 g strong flour
8 g caster sugar
2 g salt
3 eggs
25 g cocoa powder
75 g unsalted butter, softened

LIME SYRUP
juice and rind of 6 limes
200 g sugar

MAKE THE SAVARIN. Warm the milk to 37°C/100°F and then pour it over the yeast. Cover the bowl with clingfilm and leave the yeast to dissolve. Put the flour, sugar, salt and eggs into a mixing machine with a dough hook attachment and slowly add the milk and yeast mixture. Allow the machine to work the dough on a very low speed for a minimum of 10 minutes. Slowly add the butter in small amounts, waiting for it to be fully incorporated before you add the next piece. Leave the machine working the dough for another 5 minutes on slow.

COVER THE BOWL with clingfilm and leave to prove in a warm place (next to your oven is ideal) until the mixture has doubled in size. Remove the mixture from the bowl and, on a floured surface, knock all the air back out of the mix. Line four savarin moulds with butter and sugar. Roll the savarin mix into four thin sausages shapes and lay them in the savarin moulds. Cover with clingfilm and leave to prove until they double in size for a second time. Remove the clingfilm and bake in a preheated oven at 190°C/375°F/gas 5 for 15 minutes. Turn them out of the moulds immediately and place on a wire rack to cool.

MAKE THE LIME syrup by boiling the lime juice and rind with the sugar in 400 ml water. Leave to infuse for 30 minutes.

TO SERVE, dip the savarins briefly in the lime syrup. Scoop balls of the candied ginger ice cream and put into the middle of the savarins. Spoon the remaining lime syrup over the ice cream.

This is quite an unusual combination of flavours, but I love the saltiness of the goats' cheese in amongst all the sweetness.

Warm Pistachio Cake, Cherry Sorbet and Goats' Cheese Mousse

SERVES 4
1 quantity cherry sorbet
  (see page 219)
1 packet of filo pastry

PISTACHIO CAKE
200 g unsalted butter
250 g caster sugar
4 eggs
200 g ground almonds
50 g pistachio purée
50 g plain flour

POACHED CHERRIES
200 g fresh cherries
200 g caster sugar
juice and rind of 1 lemon

CHERRY BRANDY JELLY
6 poached cherries (see above)
100 ml cherry poaching liquor
  (see above)
100 ml cherry brandy
2 leaves gelatine, softened

PISTACHIO MOUSSE
200 ml crème anglaise
  (see page 216)
150 g pistachio paste
1½ leaves gelatine, softened
100 ml double cream, semi-
  whipped

GOATS' CHEESE MOUSSE
50 ml milk
125 g goats' cheese
1 leaf gelatine, softened
50 ml double cream, semi-whipped

MAKE THE CHERRY SORBET and keep it in the freezer.

PREPARE AND COOK THE FILO PASTRY as in the Fig and Filo Tart, page 164, but omitting the figs. When the pastry is cooked and while it is still warm, cut it into rectangles about 20 cm long and 1.5 cm wide. You will need eight pieces altogether.

MAKE THE PISTACHIO CAKE. Beat together the butter and sugar, then add the eggs one at a time. Add the ground almonds and the pistachio paste and finally fold in the flour. Line a 3 cm deep cake tin with greaseproof paper, pour in the mixture and cook in a preheated oven at 160°C/310°F/gas 2½ for about 35 minutes. Leave the cake to cool in the tin, then turn it out onto a wire rack and set aside.

POACH THE CHERRIES. Remove the stones with a cherry stoner. Bring 400 ml water to the boil with the sugar and lemon juice and rind. Reduce the heat, add the cherries and allow them to simmer for 2 minutes. Leave them to cool.

MAKE THE CHERRY brandy jelly. Put six of the poached cherries, the poaching liquor and the cherry brandy in a blender and blend until smooth. Pass through a fine sieve. Melt the gelatine in a little of the blended liquor on the stove and return to the liquid. Pour this into a small mould and set in the refrigerator and leave for at least 2 hours to set fully. Turn out the jelly onto a clean chopping board and cut it into 1 cm cubes. Keep refrigerated.

MAKE THE PISTACHIO MOUSSE. Warm the crème anglaise slightly and whisk in the pistachio paste. Set 4 tablespoons of this aside for dressing the plates. Add the gelatine to the remaining mixture, pass it through a fine sieve and allow to cool. Once set, fold in the cream, transfer the mixture to a piping bag and keep refrigerated until needed.

MAKE THE GOATS' CHEESE mousse. Warm the milk, add the gelatine and leave until dissolved. Blend the goats' cheese in a food processor until smooth and whisk this into the warmed milk. Once the cheese and milk are mixed together fold in the cream and keep refrigerated.

TO SERVE, cut the pistachio cake into 3 cm cubes and reheat in a warm oven for a couple of minutes. Meanwhile, spoon the pistachio-flavoured crème anglaise onto four plates, scatter the diced jelly around and add a few poached cherries. Spoon on the goats' cheese mousse, add the warmed pistachio cubes and the cherry sorbet. Finally, pipe the pistachio mousse onto four filo strips and sandwich with the remaining strips and place these on the plates. Sprinkle with grated lemon rind.

The inspiration for the recipe was the combination of strawberries and cracked black pepper. Red peppers are naturally sweet, so the combination seemed very natural. You need to make the parfait 24 hours ahead.

Strawberry and Red Pepper

SERVES 4
2 tablespoons olive oil
1 teaspoon smoked sweet paprika
12 whole strawberries
1 quantity red pepper crumbs
  (see page 214)
1 bunch of baby basil, to decorate

STRAWBERRY PARFAIT
450 g strawberries, hulled
175 g caster sugar
2 tablespoons strawberry liqueur
6 egg yolks
350 ml double cream, whipped

STRAWBERRY FOAM
200 g caster sugar
juice of 2 limes
150 g wild strawberries
3 leaves gelatine, softened

RED PEPPER CASSONADE
4 red peppers
250 g strawberries
1 vanilla pod
500 ml double cream
8 egg yolks
110 g caster sugar
4½ leaves gelatine, softened
1 teaspoon pickled pink
  peppercorns

RED PEPPER PURÉE
3 red peppers (see above)
juice of 1 lemon
2 tablespoons caster sugar
2 tablespoons strawberry liqueur

RED PEPPER TUILE
300 g red pepper purée (see above)
60 g caster sugar

MAKE THE STRAWBERRY parfait. Put the strawberries in a saucepan with 75 g sugar and the strawberry liqueur, cover and cook for 10 minutes or until the strawberries are soft. Transfer to a blender and blend until smooth. (I tend not to pass this purée through a sieve because I like the seeds the strawberries leave behind, but you can sieve the mixture if you wish.) Leave to cool.

MEANWHILE, whisk the egg yolks and the remaining sugar to firm, white ribbon stage. Fold the egg yolk mixture into the cold strawberry purée, then fold in the cream. Line a deep baking tin with greaseproof paper and pour the mixture in to a depth of 3 cm. Cover with clingfilm and freeze overnight. Cut the frozen parfait into 3 cm cubes and keep in the freezer until needed.

MAKE THE STRAWBERRY FOAM. Put the sugar, lime juice and wild strawberries in a saucepan with 200 ml water. Bring to the boil, then leave to infuse, off the heat, for 1 hour. Transfer to a blender and blend until smooth. Pass through a fine sieve. Reheat a small amount of the liquor, add the gelatine and stir until it has dissolved. Add this mixture to the strawberry liquor and allow to set in a bowl over iced water. Once set spoon into a gas canister, charge with two cartridges and give a good shake for at least 1 minute. Store in the refrigerator until needed. If you don't have a gas canister, use the mixture as a jelly rather than a foam.

MAKE THE CASSONADE. Roast all four red peppers over an open flame until they are completely black. Put them in a freezer bag for about 5 minutes to allow them to sweat then scrape away the skin. Rinse the peppers thoroughly in cold water and set aside three of them (for the purée). Remove the core and deseed the remaining pepper and finely dice the flesh. Leave it to dry on kitchen paper.

PUT THE STRAWBERRIES in a pan and cook until soft. Blend in a blender and set aside. Put the cream and the seeds from the vanilla pod in a saucepan and heat to boiling point. Mix together the egg yolks and sugar until they reach a white, creamy consistency. Slowly add the boiling cream. When the cream is fully incorporated return the mixture

back to the pan and cook over a very low heat, stirring continuously with a wooden spoon, until the mixture coats the back of the spoon. Add the gelatine and mix thoroughly.

ALLOW TO COOL SLIGHTLY, then add the diced pepper, strawberry purée and pink peppercorns. Transfer to a container and refrigerate for at least 3 hours. When it is set put the cassonade in a piping bag and keep refrigerated.

MAKE THE PURÉE. Chop the three skinned red peppers (see above) fairly coarsely, put them in a pan with the lemon juice, sugar and liqueur. Cook slowly until all the liquid has evaporated. Transfer to a blender and blend until smooth, pass the purée through a fine sieve and set aside.

MAKE THE TUILES. Take 300 g of the purée (reserving the remainder for serving) and mix it with the sugar. Spread the mixture onto an ovenproof rubber mat as thinly as possible and put it in a preheated oven at 100°C/200°F/gas ¼ overnight. Cut the dried mixture with scissors into four pieces, each about 11 x 8 cm. Wrap these around a cylinder mould to make cannelloni-like tubes and leave to set.

IN A HOT FRYING PAN gently heat the oil and smoked paprika. Add the strawberries and cook until slightly soft. Arrange the strawberries on four plates. Pipe cassonade onto the plates. Roll the parfait cubes in the red pepper crumbs and place two cubes on each plate. Fill the red pepper tuiles with the strawberry foam (or jelly) and place one on each plate. Spoon a little of the remaining red pepper purée onto the plates and decorate with basil leaves.

Adding malt extract to the mousse gives it a wonderfully rich flavour – it works perfectly with chocolate. If you can't find malt extract you can replace it with 150 g of a malt-based drink, such as Horlicks.

Malted Chocolate Mousse with Yogurt Sorbet and Hazelnut Sponge

SERVES 4
1 quantity yogurt sorbet
  (see page 219)

HAZELNUT SPONGE
3 egg whites
100 g caster sugar
2 eggs
20 g plain flour
50 g ground hazelnuts
20 g unsalted butter, melted

HAZELNUT BUTTERCREAM
½ egg
1 egg yolk
50 g caster sugar
125 g soft unsalted butter
60 g hazelnut paste
rind of ½ lime

MALTED CHOCOLATE MOUSSE
30 g unsalted butter, softened
20 g cocoa powder
1 egg yolk
20 g caster sugar
10 g malt extract
15 g plain, dark chocolate, melted
50 ml double cream, semi-whipped

MAKE THE YOGURT SORBET and keep in the freezer until needed.

MAKE THE HAZELNUT SPONGE. Whip the egg white with 50 g sugar. In a separate bowl mix together the eggs, flour, ground hazelnuts and butter. Mix a third of the meringue into the sponge mixture and mix to incorporate fully. Continue to fold the meringue in, a third at a time, making sure that you do this as lightly as possible to keep as much of the air in the mixture as you can. Pour this mixture onto a baking sheet lined with greaseproof paper and cook in a preheated oven at 180°C/350°/gas 4 for 7 minutes. Leave the sponge to cool on the tray.

MAKE THE HAZELNUT BUTTERCREAM. Whisk together the egg and egg yolk to a light mousse consistency. Boil the sugar in 20 ml water to 117°C/225°F, then pour the hot sugar mixture over the eggs and whisk until cold. Add the butter and continue to whisk until white and smooth, then mix in the hazelnut paste and lime rind.

SLICE THE HAZELNUT sponge into three equal pieces and spread half the buttercream over the top of one of them. Place another sponge on top and spread the remaining buttercream on top of this. Top with the third sponge. Transfer to the refrigerator to allow the buttercream to set.

MEANWHILE, make the malted chocolate mousse. Mix together the butter and cocoa powder. In a separate bowl whisk together the eggs, sugar and malt extract until it reaches a firm sabayon stage. Fold in the butter (do this quickly so that the butter does not set), then add the melted chocolate and cream. Transfer to a container and refrigerate for a couple of hours or until set.

TO SERVE, slice the sponge cake into four rectangles and arrange them on four plates. Spoon the yogurt sorbet and malted chocolate mousse over the sponge.

I learnt how to make this recipe while I was working at Adlard's restaurant in Norwich. Over the years the dish has evolved from a simple slice of cake to what it is now.

Orange and Olive Oil Cake with Candied Celery

SERVES 4
1 quantity orange sorbet
  (see page 219)

ORANGE PURÉE
2 oranges
150 g caster sugar
150 grams of water

ORANGE TUILE
40 g caster sugar
200 g orange purée (see above)

CAKE
30 g baking powder
30 g dried breadcrumbs
75 g ground almonds
150 g caster sugar
rind of 2 oranges
3 eggs
150 g olive oil

ORANGE JELLY
500 ml orange juice
200 g caster sugar
3½ leaves gelatine, softened
1 vanilla pod

CANDIED CELERY
6 large sticks of celery
200 g caster sugar
12 cardamom pods
1 lemon peel

MAKE THE PURÉE. Cut the oranges (unpeeled) into small pieces and put them in a saucepan with the sugar and 150 ml water. Simmer until the skins are soft and half the water has evaporated. Transfer to a blender, blend until smooth, then pass through a fine sieve.

MAKE THE TUILES. Mix together the sugar and orange purée. Spread the mixture thinly as possible on an ovenproof rubber mat and leave to dry in a preheated oven at 100°C/200°F/gas ¼ overnight. When the mixture is dry roll it around a piece of stainless steel piping to make cannelloni-like shapes.

MAKE THE CAKE. Mix together all the dry ingredients in a food processor. Add the eggs and then gradually add the olive oil keeping the machine running at a slow speed. Pour the mixture into a deep cake tin lined with greaseproof paper and cook in a preheated oven at 150°C/300°F/gas 2 for about 25 minutes. Allow the sponge to cool in the tin, then turn it out onto a wire rack. Cut the sponge into four pieces, each about 1 cm long and 3 cm wide. Line four moulds the same size as the cake with clingfilm and place a piece of sponge in the bottom of each. Set aside.

MAKE THE JELLY. Gently heat a little of the orange juice in a saucepan, add the sugar, gelatine and the seeds from the vanilla pod. Heat until the sugar and gelatine have dissolved, then add this mixture to the remaining juice. Allow the mixture to set slightly, then pour the jelly into the moulds over the cake and leave to set in the refrigerator until needed.

MAKE THE CANDIED CELERY. Peel the celery and cut the sticks into 1 cm dice. Blanch briefly in boiling water and then plunge into iced water immediately. Put the sugar, cardamom pods and lemon peel in a saucepan with 400 ml water and bring to the boil to make a syrup. Add the celery and cook over a very low heat for at least 2 hours.

TO SERVE, use a small knife to remove the sponge and jelly from the moulds. Transfer them to four plates. Spoon chilled candied celery down the side, pipe orange sorbet into the tuile tubes and arrange them on top of the celery.

This is the perfect winter dessert that is really quite simple to prepare.
I like to break the wafers into more interesting irregular shapes.

Warm Chestnut Cake
with Chocolate Sorbet

SERVES 4
1 quantity chocolate sorbet
  (see page 218)
4 fresh chestnuts, peeled
  and sliced
12 fresh cobnuts or hazelnuts,
  peeled
4 good-quality wafer biscuits

CHESTNUT GANACHE
125 ml double cream
110 g bitter chocolate
45 g unsalted butter
60 g chestnut purée

CHESTNUT CAKE
250 g bitter chocolate
250 g unsalted butter
5 eggs
200 g caster sugar
200 g plain flour
7 g baking powder

BUTTERSCOTCH SAUCE
225 g caster sugar
15 g unsalted butter
500 g double cream

MAKE THE CHOCOLATE SORBET (see page 218) and keep it in the freezer until you are ready to serve.

MAKE THE CHESTNUT GANACHE. Put all the ingredients in a saucepan and heat slowly, stirring continuously until they are all fully emulsified and incorporated.

MAKE THE CHESTNUT CAKE. Melt the chocolate and butter slowly together in a bowl over hot water. In a separate stainless steel or glass bowl whisk together the eggs and sugar over a pan of boiling water until the mixture reaches a sabayon stage (the mixture will hold firm for at least 10 seconds when cooked). Take care that you do not scramble the mixture by leaving it over the heat for too long. Once the sabayon is firm pour the melted chocolate and butter into the sabayon mixture and fold it in. Sift the flour and the baking powder over this mixture and mix in well. Pour the mixture into a piping bag and refrigerate.

MELT A LITTLE BUTTER and use a pastry brush to coat six moulds. (I always prepare one or two extra cakes when I'm cooking this recipe to allow for casualties.) Line the moulds with sugar, making sure that the sugar has covered all the butter. Stand the moulds directly on a baking tray and pipe the cake mixture into the moulds, taking care that they are only half full. Spoon in a small amount of the ganache mixture, then fill the remainder of the mould with the cake mixture. This can be kept in the refrigerator until you are ready to cook them.

MAKE THE BUTTERSCOTCH SAUCE. Heat the sugar and 50 ml water in a pan and cook until golden brown. Add the butter. Be careful because the caramel will spit. Add the cream and stir until fully incorporated. Pass through a fine sieve and chill.

COOK THE CHESTNUT cakes in a preheated oven at 190°C/375°F/gas 5 and cook for 8–10 minutes. Remove from the oven and use a palette knife to transfer them to four plates. Spoon chocolate sorbet next to the cakes, and decorate the plates with chestnuts, cobnuts or hazelnuts, butterscotch sauce and wafers.

I love cheesecake – the combination of the sweet, crumbly base with a tart, yet creamy topping is wonderful. It also works all year round. The chilli jelly is an exciting twist that we came up with in the restaurant – do leave it out if you prefer.

Lime Cheesecake with Chilli Jelly and Mangoes

SERVES 4
borage leaves or baby coriander
  leaves, to decorate

MANGO PURÉE
4 fresh, ripe mangoes
100 g sugar
juice of 1 lemon

MANGO TUILE
300 g mango purée (see above)
40 g caster sugar

MANGO SORBET
300 g mango purée (see above)
30 g caster sugar

LIME CHEESECAKE
15 plain digestive biscuits
100 g unsalted butter, melted
250 g smooth cream cheese
rind of 2 limes
50 g caster sugar
2 egg yolks
juice of 5 limes
2½ leaves gelatine, softened
250 g double cream

LIME FOAM
200 ml lime juice
150 g caster sugar
3½ leaves gelatine, softened

CHILLI JELLY
1 red chilli
75 g caster sugar
juice of 1 lemon
2 leaves gelatine, softened

MAKE THE MANGO PURÉE. Peel one of the mangoes and use a mandolin to cut eight slices as thinly as possible. Set these to one side. Peel the remaining mangoes and chop the flesh as finely as possible. Put the sugar in a saucepan with 100 ml water, bring to the boil and add the mango. Cook until the mango flesh is completely soft, then blend in a blender until smooth. Pass through a fine sieve and add the lemon juice to taste. This will give you 600 g of mango purée.

MAKE THE TUILES. Mix together the mango purée and sugar, then spread it onto an ovenproof rubber mat as thinly as possible. Leave it in a preheated oven at 100°C/200°F/gas ¼ overnight. Cut out rectangles 8 cm long and 6 cm wide and wrap them around moulds the same size as the ones you will be using for the cheesecake and leave to stand until the tuile becomes crisp. Set the remaining mango purée aside for garnishing the plates.

MAKE THE MANGO SORBET. Blend the mango in a blender with the sugar and 180 ml water. Pass the mixture through a fine sieve, churn in an ice cream machine and freeze until needed.

MAKE THE CHEESECAKE. Crush the digestive biscuits and mix the crumbs with the melted butter. Put four cylinder moulds, 5 cm across and 6 cm high, on a baking tray and spoon the biscuit mixture into the bottom of the moulds, pressing down on the mixture to form a firm base. Place in the refrigerator to set.

BEAT TOGETHER the cream cheese and lime rind until smooth. Boil 50 ml water with the sugar to 117°C/225°F. Whisk the egg yolks until they are light and creamy, then gradually add the sugar mixture and continue whisking until the mixture has cooled. Heat the lime juice slightly on the stove and dissolve the gelatine in the juice. Add the juice to the egg mixture and then add this to the cream cheese. Mix until incorporated and smooth. Semi-whip the cream and fold it into the mixture and then spoon it into the moulds. Leave to set for at least 3 hours.

MAKE THE LIME FOAM. Put the lime juice, sugar and 150 ml water in a saucepan, bring to the boil and add the gelatine. Pass through a fine

sieve and chill over a bowl of iced water. When the mixture has set, transfer it to a gas canister and charge with two gas cartridges. Keep refrigerated. If you are not using a gas canister, use the mixture as a jelly, rather than a foam.

MAKE THE CHILLI JELLY. Chop the chilli very finely and put it in a pan with the sugar, lemon juice and 200 ml water. Bring to the boil and leave to infuse off the heat for 20 minutes. Mix the gelatine into the warm mixture, then pass it through a fine sieve into a small container. Refrigerate. When the jelly is set cut it into very small dice.

TO SERVE, place the cheesecakes onto four plates and spoon the remaining mango purée and the chilli jelly onto the plates. Fill the mango tuiles with lime foam and top the mango slices with a little of the lime foam. Spoon the sorbet on top of the cheesecakes and decorate with some borage flowers or coriander leaves, if liked.

Strawberries are often paired with other strong flavours such as balsamic vinegar and peppercorns. Here, I've created a zesty lime parfait as well as a basil flavoured panna cotta to bring out the fantastic strawberry flavour. Start this recipe a day in advance.

Strawberry Jelly with Wild Strawberry Sorbet and Basil Panna Cotta

SERVES 4
1 quantity wild strawberry sorbet
  (see page 219)
baby basil leaves, to decorate

LIME PARFAIT
50 ml milk
40 g caster sugar
2 egg yolks
1/2 leaf gelatine, softened
50 ml lime juice, reduced by half
grated rind of 1/2 lime
75 ml double cream, semi-whipped

STRAWBERRY JELLY
200 g strawberries, hulled
250 grams of water
250 g caster sugar
juice of 2 limes
1 vanilla pod
3 1/2 leaves of gelatine, softened

BASIL PANNA COTTA
200 ml double cream
60 g caster sugar
2 bunches of picked basil leaves
2 1/2 leaves of gelatine, softened
200 ml of cold milk

MAKE THE WILD STRAWBERRY sorbet (see page 219) and keep it in the freezer until you are ready to serve.

MAKE THE LIME PARFAIT. Put the milk and half the sugar in a saucepan and bring to the boil. Whisk the egg yolks and the remaining sugar together until they become creamy and white. Gradually and gently pour the boiling milk over the egg mixture and whisk until fully incorporated. Return to the pan and reheat to the first bubble (boil). Add the gelatine and when this has dissolved, pass the mixture though a fine sieve and into a large bowl sitting in iced water. Add the lime juice and rind and leave until the mixture sets. When it is firm fold in the cream until thoroughly mixed. Pour the mixture into a stainless steel tray 2 cm deep and freeze overnight. When the parfait is frozen cut it into 2 cm cubes and refreeze.

MAKE THE STRAWBERRY JELLY. Slice the strawberries fairly finely and put them in a saucepan with the sugar, lime juice, vanilla pod and 250 ml water. Bring to a slow boil, remove from the stove and leave to infuse for 1 hour. Pass through a fine sieve. Reheat a little of the liquor in a small pan and add the gelatine. When the gelatine has dissolved, return the mixture to the strawberry mixture, pour into a bowl and allow to set in the refrigerator for at least 1 hour.

MAKE THE BASIL panna cotta. Put the cream and sugar in a pan and heat together. Add the basil leaves, reboil and transfer to a blender. Blend until smooth, adding the gelatine while the mixture is still in the blender. Pass the basil sauce through a fine sieve into a bowl sitting over iced water. Mix in the cold milk and leave to set.

TO SERVE, spoon the basil panna cotta into four large chilled glasses, spoon on the cubes of lime parfait, followed by the strawberry jelly, strawberry sorbet and finally some baby basil.

Fundamentals

Artichoke Cooking Liquor

MAKES 475 ML
1 head of garlic, peeled
  and roughly chopped
3 large shallots, peeled
  and roughly chopped
100 ml olive oil
300 ml water
75 ml white wine vinegar
1 teaspoon vitamin C powder
10 large sprigs of thyme
10 peppercorns
salt and pepper

GENTLY COOK the garlic and shallot in a large saucepan with the oil, taking care that they do not colour. Add the water, vinegar and vitamin C powder and bring to the boil. Add the thyme leaves and peppercorns and bring back to the boil.

TASTE AND CHECK the seasoning (be careful because it will be very hot).

THE LIQUOR is now ready to cook your artichokes in. Make sure it is boiling hot when you add the artichokes as this helps keep them as white as possible. The liquor can be used again and again.

Vegetable Stock

MAKES 3 LITRES
5 carrots, peeled
2 onions, peeled
2 celery sticks
1 leek
1 head of garlic
1 fennel bulb
3 litres water
3 bay leaves
6 sprigs of thyme
2 star anise
2 sprigs of tarragon
2 sprigs of dill
4 sprigs of chervil
6 slices of lemon
300 ml white wine

ROUGHLY CHOP the vegetables into evenly sized pieces. Put them in a large saucepan, cover with the water and add the bay leaves and thyme. Bring to the boil and simmer for 8 minutes. Add the remaining herbs and simmer for a couple more minutes.

ADD THE LEMON slices and the white wine, remove from the heat and allow to cool.

PASS THE COOL liquid through a fine sieve and either use it immediately or freeze it. Alternatively, you can keep the mixture in the refrigerator before straining it for no more than 2 days.

White Chicken Stock

MAKES 3 LITRES
10 kg chicken wings
5 litres cold water
1 leek (white part only)
2 celery sticks
2 white onions, peeled
1 heads of garlic
½ bunch of thyme
2 tablespoons rock salt
10 white peppercorns
6 bay leaves

PUT THE CHICKEN wings in a large saucepan, cover with the water and bring to the boil, removing any excess fat that rises to the top. Simmer for 30 minutes, skimming continuously to remove all the fat.

MEANWHILE, chop the vegetables fairly roughly and add them to the saucepan. Add the salt, peppercorns and bay leaves and cook for at least 6 hours at a gentle simmer.

WHEN THE STOCK is cooked remove the bones and vegetables and pass the stock through a fine sieve. Leave to cool, then refrigerate or freeze.

Brown Chicken Stock

MAKES 3 LITRES
5 kg chicken wings
500 g carrots
1 bulb of garlic
500 g white onions
¼ bunch of thyme
8 white peppercorns
1 tablespoon rock salt
75 ml vegetable oil
100 g butter, diced
5 litres white chicken stock
  (see above)

CHOP EACH CHICKEN wing into three or four pieces. Chop the vegetables fairly roughly, keeping them all separate.

HEAT A LARGE roasting tray in a preheated oven at 200°C/400°F/gas 6. Carefully pour half the oil into the tray and return to the oven for 5 minutes so that the oil gets extremely hot.

PUT THE CHICKEN wings into the oil, spreading them evenly in the tin. Cook the wings until they are golden brown all over, occasionally turning them with a wooden spoon.

MEANWHILE, in a hot heavy casserole heat the remaining oil, add the butter and wait until it starts to foam (take care not to let it burn). Add the chopped carrots and garlic and caramelize evenly. Then add the chopped onion, thyme and peppercorns and caramelize for a further 5–10 minutes. Once all the vegetables are golden brown drain the butter and oil away and return the vegetables to the pan.

DRAIN THE OIL away from the roasted chicken wings (use a colander for this) and add the wings to the vegetables.

COVER WITH white chicken stock, adding the salt and white peppercorns. Bring to the boil and skim any excess fat from the top. Simmer for at least 6 hours, skimming occasionally.

PASS THE STOCK through a fine sieve and reduce to the consistency you require.

Crayfish Stock

MAKES 1 LITRE
200 ml olive oil
500 grams langoustine or
  crayfish shells
2 fennel bulbs, roughly chopped
4 large shallots, roughly chopped
4 star anise
1/2 head of garlic
4 large sprigs of tarragon
6 white peppercorns

PREHEAT THE OVEN to 180°C/350°F/gas 4 and place the oil in a large roasting tin to heat up. Carefully put the shells in the hot olive oil and spread them evenly around the tray. Roast for 15–20 minutes, turning them occasionally with a wooden spoon.

DRAIN AWAY the oil (you can use it to dress a salad later). Put the bones in a large casserole pan with the chopped vegetables, herbs and spices and cover with the cold water. Bring to the boil and cook for 1½ hours. Pass it through a fine sieve, then either refrigerate or freeze.

Fish Stock

MAKES 2 LITRES
1.5 kg good quality white fish
  bones, such as turbot, sole
  or plaice
50 ml olive oil
2 fennel bulbs, chopped
6 large shallots, chopped
200 ml white wine
4 bay leaves
6 large sprigs of thyme
6 large sprigs of tarragon
1/2 bunch of chervil
10 large sprigs of flat leaf parsley
10 white peppercorns

REMOVE THE GILLS, guts and eyes (anything that contains blood) from the fish bones. Chop the bones into fairly small pieces and run them under cold water for at least an hour to rinse any excess blood away.

HEAT THE OIL in a large casserole pan and add the drained fish bones. Cover and sweat for 2–3 minutes. Add the chopped vegetables and the white wine and reduce until the bones are almost dry.

COVER THE BONES with ice cubes and bring to the boil (this will help clarify the stock). When the ice has melted add the fresh herbs and peppercorns, skim any grease from the surface, turn down the heat to a simmer and cook for 20 minutes.

ALLOW THE STOCK to cool with the bones still in and then pass through a fine sieve, taking care that you do not disturb the sediment in the bottom of the pan. You can keep the stock in the refrigerator for up to 2 days or freeze.

Lamb Stock

MAKES 1.5 LITRES
5 kg lamb bones (keeping
  the lamb fat separate)
500 g carrots, peeled
500 g onions, peeled
1 head of garlic
75 g overripe tomatoes
75 ml vegetable oil
1.5 litres white chicken stock
  (see page 199)
1 tablespoon tomato purée
  concentrate
1/4 bunch of thyme
1 tablespoon rock salt

USE A CLEAVER or large chopping knife to chop the lamb bones fairly small. Cut the fat into fairly small dice and keep the two separate. Chop the carrots, onions, garlic and tomatoes roughly but evenly, also keeping them all separate.

HEAT A LARGE casserole pan until it is very hot. Add the vegetable oil and wait until it is almost smoking. Add the lamb fat and wait until it caramelizes, then add the chopped bones, again caramelize slightly. Add the carrots and garlic and caramelize a little more. The fat should be foaming nicely at this stage. Add the chopped onions and thyme. Caramelize and then drain the hot fat away.

COVER THE VEGETABLES and lamb fat with 500 ml cold water and half the white chicken stock. Add the tomatoes and tomato purée. Bring to the boil, skim away any excess fat grease and simmer for at least 4 hours.

ONCE COOKED, pass through a fine sieve and then through a muslin cloth. Reduce by half and set aside. Once the stock has been reduced by half it can be reduced further to take on consistency of a sauce.

Veal Stock

MAKES 5 LITRES
5 kg chopped veal knuckles
50 ml vegetable oil
1 kg carrots, peeled and halved
1 kg white onions, peeled and
  halved
1/2 head of garlic
1 tablespoons rock salt
1/2 tablespoon tomato purée
500 g overripe breakfast tomatoes
1 bunch of thyme
salt

SPRINKLE SALT over the bones and slowly roast in the oil in a preheated oven 140°C/275°F/gas 1 for about 2 hours.

PUT THE ROASTED bones in your largest casserole, leaving the oil in the roasting tray.

PUT THE CARROTS and onions in the roasting tray with the garlic. Increase the oven temperature to 180°C/350°F/gas 4 and roast the vegetables for about 1 hour until they are cooked and golden brown.

ADD THE ROASTED vegetables to the bones and cover with cold water. Add the tomato purée, the tomatoes and thyme. Bring to the boil. Skim away any fat that rises to the top and simmer for at least 6–8 hours, skimming continuously.

WHEN THE STOCK is cooked, pass it through a fine sieve and then through a muslin cloth. Reduce the stock by half over a fast heat. Set aside and refrigerate or freeze.

Asparagus Purée

MAKES 200 G
250 g asparagus
25 g butter
salt and pepper

REMOVE THE WOODY bases from the asparagus by bending each spear and allowing it to snap. The asparagus below the point where it has snapped is not edible, so throw it away.

FINELY CHOP the remaining asparagus and put it in a warm pan with the butter. Place over a medium heat, cover and allow to sweat for 4–5 minutes. Do not allow the asparagus to colour.

SEASON WITH SALT and pepper, then blend until smooth in a blender. Pass through a fine sieve into a bowl over iced water. Refrigerate until needed.

Lemon Purée

MAKES 250 G
6 whole unwaxed lemons
400 ml water
200 g caster sugar
lemon juice, to taste

CHOP THE LEMONS into four and then into four again. Put the pieces in a saucepan, add the water and bring to the boil over a medium heat. Simmer until three-quarters of the liquid has evaporated. Add the sugar and continue to cook until almost dry.

BLEND IN A BLENDER and pass through a fine sieve. Taste and either add more sugar or more fresh lemon juice. Chill and refrigerate until needed.

Watercress Purée

MAKES 100 G
400 g watercress
50 g butter
salt

PICK THE LEAVES from the watercress and shred them finely. Put them in a hot pan with the butter, season with salt, cover and cook until soft.

ONCE THE WATERCRESS is cooked transfer it to a blender and blend until smooth. Pass through a fine sieve into a bowl over iced water, then refrigerate until needed.

Green Olive and Celery Purée

MAKES 300 G
200 g pitted green olives
3 shallots, thinly sliced
50 g butter
6 cardamom pods
6 celery sticks, finely chopped
rind of 1 orange
4 large sprigs of thyme
200 ml white wine
300 ml white chicken stock
  (see page 199)
200 ml orange juice
10 marjoram leaves

CUT THE OLIVES into quarters.

SWEAT THE SHALLOTS in butter in a warm pan with the cardamom pods. Add the celery and orange rind and cook, covered, for a further 7–8 minutes or until the celery is soft. Add the green olives and thyme and sweat for a further 3 minutes.

ADD THE WHITE WINE and reduce until dry. Add the chicken stock and reduce until dry, then add the orange juice. Reduce again until dry.

ADD THE MARJORAM leaves, remove the cardamom pods and blend until very smooth. Pass through a very fine sieve.

Beetroot Purée

MAKES 250 G
300 g fresh beetroot
100 ml ruby port
150 ml apple juice
100 g caster sugar
100 ml lemon juice
salt

WASH THE BEETROOT to remove any traces of soil. Wrap each beetroot individually in foil, place them on a baking tray lined with rock salt and cook in a preheated oven at 160°C/310°F/gas 2½ for 1½ hours.

REMOVE THE BEETROOT from the oven and leave to cool in the foil before you attempt to peel them. This will allow the skin to sweat, making them easier and less messy to peel.

PEEL THE BEETROOT and chop each one into eight pieces. Put them in a saucepan with the ruby port and apple juice and leave to marinade overnight.

HEAT THE MIXTURE, simmering until the liquid has reduced by two-thirds. While it is still hot blend in a blender until smooth. While the mixture is still in the blender add the sugar and lemon juice and season with salt. Pass through a fine sieve into a bowl over iced water. When it is cool refrigerate until needed.

Béchamel Sauce

MAKES 750 ML
750 ml whole milk
2 bay leaves
10 peppercorns
4 sprigs of thyme
1/2 onion
50 g butter
50 g plain flour
salt

HEAT THE MILK with the bay leaves, peppercorns, thyme and onion.

MELT THE BUTTER in a heavy-bottomed saucepan and, over medium heat, gradually beat in the flour with a wooden spoon. When the flour is fully incorporated gradually add the warm milk, using a whisk to mix it smoothly.

WHEN ALL THE MILK has been add, use a wooden spoon to beat the sauce to give a shiny, velvety texture. While it is still hot, pass the sauce through a fine sieve, season with salt and allow to cool, placing a piece of buttered greaseproof paper on top to stop a skin forming.

Potato Gnocchi

MAKES ABOUT 6 PORTIONS
700 g Desiree potatoes
2 egg yolks
90 g 'oo' strong flour
10 g potato starch (fecule)
olive oil
salt and pepper

BAKE THE POTATOES IN THEIR SKINS. They need to be just cooked, so take care that you do not over- or undercook them. Remove the flesh and put through a mouli.

PUT THE POTATO (you should have about 400 g) into a bowl, add the egg yolks, flour and potato starch and season. Mix well. Divide the mixture into four and roll out each piece, coating it in flour, into a long sausage shape 3–4 mm in diameter. Cut each sausage into 2-cm lengths so they are like little barrels. Put them on a tray.

ADD A LITTLE SALT and olive oil to a saucepan of water and bring to the boil. Turn down to simmer and the gnocchi. When they float to the top remove them from the pan into iced water to cool.

ONCE THE GNOCCHI have cooled, drain and place them on a tray with a little olive oil to prevent them from sticking.

Pasta

MAKES ABOUT 1.4 KG
9 eggs
1.1 kg 'oo' pasta flour
olive oil

FIT A DOUGH hook to your machine. Whisk the eggs and gradually add the flour. Add a dash of olive oil, keeping the mixture as dry as possible.

FEED THE PASTA through a pasta machine, working the pasta for about 10 minutes.

IF YOU ARE NOT using the pasta straight away, roll it through the pasta machine in even sized pieces, wrap it tightly in clingfilm and freeze until it is needed.

Ricotta Gnocchi

MAKES ABOUT 20 GNOCCHI
500 g ricotta
50 g 'oo' flour
2 egg yolks
1 whole egg
olive oil
salt and pepper

MIX THE RICOTTA with the flour and egg yolks and the whole egg. Season.

BRING A PAN of water to the boil and add a little salt and olive oil. Drop individual spoonfuls of the ricotta mix into the water. When they start to float they are ready and can be transferred to a bowl of iced water to cool. Leave in the iced water for no more than a minute as they will fall apart if they are left to long in the water.

TRANSFER TO a tray greased with a little olive oil to prevent them from sticking.

Risotto Base

MAKES 250 G
100 g shallots, finely chopped
4 sprigs of thyme
50 g butter
200 g arborio or carnaroli rice
200 ml white wine
1 litre hot white chicken stock
  (see page 199)
salt and pepper

PUT THE SHALLOTS and thyme leaves in a large saucepan with the butter and cook over a medium heat until the shallots are soft.

STIR IN the rice and cook over a gentle heat for a minute or so. Add the white wine and cook slowly, stirring continuously, until the wine has been absorbed by the rice.

GRADUALLY ADD the hot stock, a small ladle at a time, stirring continuously and waiting for the stock to be absorbed before you add another ladleful. When all the stock has been added and absorbed the risotto should be cooked.

WHILE THE RICE is still warm season with salt and pepper. Transfer to a large, cold metal tray, cover with greaseproof paper and refrigerate until you need it.

Mashed Potato

MAKES 1 KG
5 large red-skinned Desiree
  potatoes
75 g cold butter, diced
50 ml warm milk
100 g rock salt

BAKE THE POTATOES in their jackets until you can pierce the flesh easily with a knife. Wear kitchen gloves to cut the potatoes in half and spoon out the insides.

WHILE THE POTATO is still hot, pass it through a fine sieve and then, with a wooden spoon, start adding the butter into the potato. Avoid over-mixing the potatoes because the starch will be released and the mash will become like wallpaper paste.

WHEN THE BUTTER is fully incorporated slowly fold in the warm milk. Season with salt and almost any other ingredient you like, depending on what you are cooking.

Shallot Confit

MAKES 300 G
1.5 kg finely chopped shallots,
  finely chopped
100 g butter, diced
3 tablespoons thyme leaves
salt

PUT ALL THE ingredients in a large, heatproof casserole, season with salt, cover and allow to sweat over a low heat for 15 minutes.

REMOVE THE LID from the pan and cook for a further 15 minutes or until all the liquid from the shallots has evaporated. Allow to cool and then refrigerate until needed.

Tomato Confit

MAKES 40 PIECES
10 plum tomatoes
100 ml olive oil
10 sprigs of thyme
2 garlic cloves
25 g icing sugar

BLANCH THE TOMATOES in boiling salted water for no more than 10 seconds. Remove from the water and plunge into iced water before peeling. Cut the flesh into quarters lengthways and use a small knife to remove the hearts.

PUT THE TOMATO flesh on a wire rack. Drizzle over the olive oil and sprinkle over the thyme leaves.

FINELY SLICE the garlic and lay one slither of garlic on each piece of tomato. Transfer to the oven, set at 100°C/200°F/gas ¼, and leave to dry overnight. Refrigerate until needed.

Sweet Red Pepper Vinaigrette

MAKES 100 ML
6 whole red peppers
75 ml lemon juice
100 ml olive oil
caster sugar
salt

CORE AND DESEED the red peppers. Pass the flesh through a vegetable juicer and then through a fine sieve. Put the juice in a saucepan and bring to the boil. Skim away any excess sediment and then pass through a muslin cloth.

RETURN TO THE HEAT and reduce the juice until it almost resembles syrup. Allow to cool, season with the lemon juice and a little salt and sugar if necessary. Finally add the olive oil.

Orange Vinaigrette

MAKES 800 ML
30 g caster sugar
500 ml fresh orange juice (from
    about 5 oranges)
10 g orange rind
100 ml white wine vinegar
400 ml sunflower oil

DISSOLVE THE SUGAR in the orange juice, add 100 ml water and the orange rind and reduce to approximately 200 ml.

TRANSFER TO A BLENDER and, while the blender is running, slowly add the oil. Add a little more water if it gets too thick.

Truffle Vinaigrette

MAKES 900 G
600 g shallots, finely chopped
3 tablespoons picked thyme leaves
50 g butter
600 g cheap Chinese truffles,
    finely chopped
1/2 bottle of Madeira
150 ml balsamic vinegar
125 ml white truffle oil
salt

SWEAT THE SHALLOTS and thyme in the butter until they are soft, add the truffle and cook for a further 2 minutes.

ADD THE MADEIRA and cook to reduce until almost dry. Repeat the process with the balsamic vinegar.

REMOVE THE PAN from the heat, add the truffle oil and season with salt. Allow to cool.

Red Wine Sauce

MAKES 250 ML
300 g shallots
1 heads of garlic
1 bottles of red wine
1 bottles of ruby port
1/2 bunch of thyme
300 ml veal stock (see page 202)
300 ml litres brown chicken stock
    (see page 199)

PEEL AND CHOP the shallots roughly and cut the garlic in half widthways. Cover with the red wine and port, add the thyme and leave to marinade for 24 hours.

COOK THE LIQUID and the shallots on the stove and reduce by two-thirds on a fast heat.

ADD THE VEAL and brown chicken stock and simmer for 2 hours, occasionally skimming away any excess sediment. Pass through a fine sieve and then through muslin.

REDUCE TO your required consistency. Check the seasoning. You may need a little sugar.

Sweet Garlic Butter Sauce

MAKES 200 ML
6 garlic cloves
100 ml duck fat
50 shallots, finely chopped
150 g cold butter, diced
100 ml white wine vinegar
100 ml sweet white wine
4 large sprigs of thyme
salt

PEEL THE GARLIC and put the cloves in a casserole dish with the duck fat and thyme. Cook over a low heat for 3 hours or until the garlic cloves are soft.

SWEAT THE SHALLOTS in a knob of butter without letting them colour, then add the cooked garlic cloves and white wine vinegar. Reduce until all the liquid has almost gone.

ADD THE SWEET white wine and reduce again until all the liquid has almost gone.

BEGIN TO WHISK in the remaining butter over a warm heat. Add the butter piece by piece, making sure that each piece is fully incorporated before adding the next. Season with a touch of salt.

KEEP WARM and covered with clingfilm in the pan until required.

Parmesan Cream Sauce

MAKES 300 ML
200 ml white wine
3 large sprigs of thyme
400 ml white chicken stock
  (see page 199)
100 ml double cream
3 tablespoons very finely grated
  Parmesan cheese

PUT THE WHITE WINE and thyme in a saucepan and cook until reduced by half. Add the stock and reduce this by half. Add the cream and again, reduce by half.

PUT THE SAUCE in a blender and add the Parmesan powder. Blend until smooth, allow to cool and refrigerate.

Truffle Cream Sauce

MAKES 350 ML
100 g black truffles
200 ml Madeira
100 ml white wine
200 ml white chicken stock
  (see page 199)
75 ml double cream
sherry vinegar
salt

CLEAN THE TRUFFLES and chop them fairly roughly. Put them in a bowl, cover with the Madeira and leave to marinade for 24 hours.

PUT THE TRUFFLES and Madeira in a small saucepan, heat to simmer and cook until the truffles are soft.

MEANWHILE, reduce the white wine by two-thirds. Add the stock and reduce by half. Add the cream and reduce again by half.

PUT THE TRUFFLES and the chicken cream in a blender and blend until smooth. The cream will become a jet black sauce and should coat the back of a spoon. Adjust the seasoning with a touch of salt and a dash of sherry vinegar.

Red Pepper Crust

MAKES 300 G
2 red peppers, skinned
juice of 1 lemon
1 tablespoon caster sugar
100 g fine breadcrumbs
75 g Gruyère cheese, grated
75 g butter, melted
salt and pepper

CHOP THE RED PEPPERS coarsely and put them in a pan with the lemon juice and sugar. Cook slowly until all the liquid has evaporated. Transfer to a blender and blend until smooth. Allow to cool and then add the breadcrumbs, grated cheese and melted butter. Blend again and season to taste.

ROLL OUT the mixture between two sheets of greaseproof paper and chill.

Red Pepper Crumbs

10 dried red peppers
50 g ground almonds
50 g fine breadcrumbs
1 garlic clove, chopped
3 slices of fresh red chilli

BLEND THE DRIED red peppers in a blender with the rest of the ingredients until very smooth. Season with a touch of salt.

Chicken Mousse

MAKES 300 G
1½ chicken breasts, trimmed of
  sinew, fat and skin and diced
1 egg white
250 ml double cream
salt

BEFORE YOU START make sure that the bowl of your food processor is chilled.

PUT THE DICED chicken in the blender and blend until very smooth. Add the egg white and blend until fully amalgamated.

CLEAN DOWN the sides of the bowl (preferably with a rubber spatula), then add two-thirds of the cream while the blender is still running.

CLEAN DOWN the sides again and add a good tablespoon of salt and the remaining cream. Blend until the mousse is a light consistency but take care that you do not overmix or the cream will separate and you will have to start again.

Pigeon Sauce/Mousse

MAKES 300 G
2 pigeon carcasses
100 g butter
2 shallots, coarsely chopped
1 clove of garlic, cut into 3
4 sprigs of thyme
5 white peppercorns
2 bay leaves
100 ml port
100 ml Madeira
500 ml brown chicken stock
 (see page 199)
30 g pigeon breast
70 g chicken breast
2 eggs
165 ml single cream
30 g diced foie gras
salt

BEFORE YOU START make sure all your ingredients are at room temperature.

CHOP THE PIGEON bones and roast them on the stove in a hot pan with 50 g of butter. Once caramelized add the chopped shallot, garlic, thyme, peppercorns and bay leaves and continue to cook. When they are all evenly caramelized, drain away the butter and add the port and Madeira and reduce until almost dry.

ADD THE STOCK, bring to the boil, skim away any 'scum' and simmer for 20–30 minutes.

PASS THE LIQUID through a fine sieve and then through a muslin. Allow to cool to room temperature. Set 300 ml of this liquid aside – this is the pigeon sauce.

REMOVE THE SKIN and sinew from the pigeon and chicken breasts and blend in a food processor until smooth. Add the remaining pigeon sauce and blend again. Add the eggs and half the cream. Add the butter and the foie gras. Then add the remaining cream. Season with salt and then pass through a fines sieve.

WHEN READY TO SERVE, these mousses can be cooked in buttered moulds covered with foil in a bain marie in a preheated oven at 80–90°C/180°F. The cooking time will depend on the size of the mould. Each mouse should be firm to the touch when cooked.

Chicken Liver Parfait

MAKES 500 G
3 large shallots, finely chopped
¼ bottle of port
¼ bottle of Madeira
200 g foie gras
200 g chicken livers
2 whole eggs
200 g butter, melted
salt

MAKE SURE THE foie gras, butter and cream are all at room temperature before you start.

SWEAT THE SHALLOTS in a little butter until they are soft, but not coloured. Add the port and Madeira to the pan, cook over a medium heat until fully absorbed by the shallots.

BRING THE REMAINING ingredients to body temperature, then blend the foie gras, livers and shallot and alcohol reduction together in the food processor until smooth.

ADD THE EGGS and blend again. Start adding the butter slowly to make an emulsion (in the same way you make a mayonnaise). Season with salt.

POUR THE MIXTURE into a lined terrine mould and bake in a bain marie at 90°C/180°F for about 45 minutes.

Crème Anglaise

MAKES 400 ML
4 egg yolks
35 g caster sugar
60 ml cream
360 ml milk

WHISK TOGETHER the egg yolks and sugar until they are smooth and creamy.

PUT THE CREAM and milk into a saucepan and bring to the boil.

POUR THE CREAM and milk over the eggs, whisking continuously. Return to the pan and cook over a low heat, stirring continuously, until the temperature reaches 73°C/163°F. Do not allow to boil.

PASS THROUGH a fine sieve, cover loosely with clingfilm and refrigerate until needed. Crème anglaise is the base for a basic ice cream. Simply churn in an ice cream machine and freeze until needed.

Burnt Honey Ice Cream

MAKES 300 ML
100 g honey
250 ml double cream
250 g caster sugar
8 egg yolks

PUT THE HONEY in a saucepan and heat until it begins to smoke very slightly. Add the cream, making sure you stand well back when you do this because it will spit and splash.

WHISK TOGETHER the sugar and egg yolks, then add the hot cream to the sugar and eggs. Return the mixture to the saucepan and cook on a low heat, stirring continuously, until the temperature reaches 84°C/183°F.

PASS THROUGH a fine sieve into a bowl sitting over iced water.

ONCE CHILLED, churn in an ice cream machine and freeze until needed.

Calvados Ice Cream

MAKES 700 ML
500 ml milk
215 ml cream
30 g milk powder
35 g glucose
1 vanilla pod
5 g of staboline (available from
  cake decorating suppliers)
130 g of sugar
3 egg yolks
Calvados to taste

PUT THE MILK, cream, milk powder, glucose and vanilla pod into a saucepan and heat slowly.

WHISK TOGETHER the staboline, sugar and egg yolks, then add the hot milk and cream to the mixture. Return to the saucepan and cook over a low heat, stirring continuously, until the temperature reaches 84°C/183°F. Stir in the Calvados.

PASS THE MIXTURE through a fine sieve into a bowl sitting over iced water.

ONCE CHILLED, churn in an ice cream machine and freeze until needed.

Candied Ginger Ice Cream

MAKES 500 ML
250 ml milk
250 ml cream
50 g candied ginger
125 g sugar
5 egg yolks

PUT THE MILK, cream and candied ginger in a saucepan and bring to the boil.

WHISK TOGETHER the sugar and the egg yolks, then pour the hot liquid over the egg yolk mixture and return to the saucepan. Cook over a low heat until it reaches 84°C/183°F.

PASS THE MIXTURE through a fine sieve into a bowl sitting over iced water.

ONCE CHILLED, churn in an ice cream machine and freeze until needed.

Palm Sugar Ice Cream

MAKES 500 ML
125 g palm sugar
250 ml milk
250 ml cream
50 g shredded coconut
5 egg yolks

PUT THE PALM SUGAR in a saucepan over a high heat. Allow the sugar to caramelize, and then add the milk and cream. Toast the shredded coconut and add quickly to the liquid. Mix thoroughly.

PASS THROUGH a fine sieve and pour directly onto the egg yolks, mixing immediately. Transfer to a clean saucepan and cook over a low heat until the mixture reaches 84°C/183°F. Allow to chill over a bowl of iced water.

CHURN IN AN ice cream machine and freeze until needed.

Chocolate Sorbet

MAKES 300 ML
250 ml milk
80 g caster sugar
40 g glucose syrup
250 g dark chocolate

PUT THE MILK, sugar and glucose in a pan and bring to the boil. Pour the mixture over the dark chocolate and mix well until fully incorporated.

CHURN IN the ice cream machine and freeze until needed.

Green Apple Sorbet

MAKES 400 ML
250 g caster sugar
300 g fresh apple juice
juice of 1 lemon
1 tablespoon staboline (available from cake decorating suppliers)
300 g green apple peelings

PLACE ALL THE INGREDIENTS into a blender with 250 ml water and blend until smooth. This will take about 1 minute depending on how powerful your blender is.

PASS THROUGH a fine sieve and transfer to an ice cream machine. Churn, then freeze immediately to help prevent the apple from discolouring.

Lime and Ginger Sorbet

MAKES 500 ML
500 ml fresh lime juice
600 g caster sugar
100 g fresh ginger

PLACE ALL THE INGREDIENTS, except half the lime juice, in a pan with 900 ml water and bring to the boil.

TRANSFER TO A BLENDER and blend until smooth. Pass through a fine sieve and add the remaining lime juice.

CHURN IN AN ICE CREAM machine and freeze until needed.

Orange Sorbet

MAKES 800 ML
300 g caster sugar
rind of 2 oranges
500 ml fresh orange juice
32 ml olive oil
juice of 2 lemons

PLACE THE SUGAR and orange rind in a saucepan with 125 ml water and bring to the boil. Add the remaining ingredients, then allow to cool over a bowl of iced water.

PASS THE MIXTURE through a fine sieve and then churn in an ice cream machine and freeze until needed.

Wild Strawberry Sorbet

MAKES 600 ML
500 g wild strawberries
500 g strawberries
300 g caster sugar
juice of 2 lemons

PUT ALL THE STRAWBERRIES in a saucepan, add 300 ml water and bring to the boil. Add the sugar and lemon juice. Transfer to a blender, blend until smooth and pour into a bowl.

CHILL OVER A BOWL of iced water, then churn in an ice cream machine and freeze until needed.

Yogurt Sorbet

MAKES 400 ML
125 g caster sugar
300 ml plain yogurt
3 tablespoons yogurt powder

PUT THE SUGAR in a saucepan with 150 ml water, bring to the boil and simmer for 5 minutes.

ALLOW THE SYRUP to cool slightly and then whisk in the yogurt and the yogurt powder.

PASS THROUGH a fine sieve into a bowl over iced water.

CHURN IN AN ice cream machine and freeze until needed.

Cherry Sorbet

MAKES 500 ML
500 g fresh cherries, pitted
200 g caster sugar
300 ml water

PLACE ALL THE INGREDIENTS in a pan and bring to the boil. Simmer for a few minutes and then remove from the heat. Transfer to a blender and blend until smooth.

PASS THROUGH a fine sieve into a bowl set over a bowl of iced water.

CHURN IN AN ice cream machine and freeze until needed.

Index

Acknowledgements

I would like to thank the following people for their involvement in my life and in this book:

First off my family, especially Mum and Dad for their continued belief in me and my brother Louis for sticking with it and becoming a great chef in his own right. Also my Auntie Doreen and Alan Feeney for putting themselves out for me when I was a young lad.

There are so many people who have helped me professionally: I thank you all. Jenny Thoden and Stewart Warner for always being by my side, Tom Aikens for his contagious inspiration and all the chefs at the Dorchester who helped me on this book: Mark Hanover, Danielle Piccinini, Luca Parente, Kieran O'Shaunessy, Sally Rickard, Binu Cherain, Rossario Sandonato, Arvind Chandran, Jared Barnes and Stephanie Morisse. A special thank you to Zoe Jenkins and Henri Brosi and everyone at the Dorchester Hotel. Thank you also to Maureen Mills at Network London for all her positive advice and Richard Vine for not only supplying the most fantastic and original produce but for also being the perfect friend.

Thanks also to everyone who has worked with me on this book – it's been an amazing adventure. I would especially like to mention Sue Atkinson for sharing the same vision as me and for taking the perfect picture, both in the kitchen and on location – particularly in freezing winds on a tiny boat out at sea! Thank you to Roisin Nield for sourcing some fantastic props. Also to all at New Holland for allowing this book to happen – especially Clare Sayer for allowing me so much freedom – and everyone at Smith & Gilmour.

First published in 2008 by New Holland Publishers (UK) Ltd
London · Cape Town · Sydney · Auckland

Garfield House, 86–88 Edgware Road, London, W2 2EA, United Kingdom
www.newhollandpublishers.com

80 McKenzie Street, Cape Town 8001, South Africa
Unit 1, 66 Gibbes Street, Chatswood, NSW 2067, Australia
218 Lake Road, Northcote, Auckland, New Zealand

1 3 5 7 9 10 8 6 4 2

ISBN 978 1 84773 160 9

Commissioning editor Clare Sayer
Photographs Sue Atkinson
Stylist Roisin Nield
Design Smith & Gilmour
Editorial Direction Rosemary Wilkinson
Production Marion Storz

Reproduction by Pica Digital PTE Ltd, Singapore
Printed and bound by Tien Wah Press Pte Ltd, Malaysia